THE TERRIBLE TWOS

A Parent's Guide

Shanta
Everington

First published in Great Britain in 2010 by
Need2Know
Remus House
Coltsfoot Drive
Peterborough
PE2 9JX
Telephone 01733 898103
Fax 01733 313524
www.need2knowbooks.co.uk

Need2Know is an imprint of Forward Press Ltd.
www.forwardpress.co.uk
SB ISBN 978-1-86144-094-5
Cover photograph: istockphoto

Contents

Introduction

You might be reading this book because your beloved son or daughter is approaching two years old and you have heard all about the terrible twos and want to know how to avoid problems. Perhaps your angelic baby seems to have turned into a monster overnight and you want some advice on what to do.

If this is your first child, you will be encountering these challenges for the first time and learning as you go along. If this is your second child, you may feel that you want to do things differently this time around.

In any event, you are not alone. Parenting at any stage is a hugely demanding job but also hugely rewarding. Parenting during the terrible twos can be a testing time. Although there may be times when you want to hurl yourself out of the nearest window, it is important to get things into perspective by remembering that all parents face challenges and there are ways to overcome them.

The first step is to understand why your child is acting the way they are. The next step is to find the right parenting strategies for you and your family.

I am a parent and qualified early years teacher. Combining my own personal experience and a wide range of family case studies with underpinning parenting theory and practical strategies, this guide will provide you with all the information and support you need to survive this potentially trying time.

You may find yourself asking questions like these:

- Why is my two-year-old suddenly saying no to everything?
- How do I get my child to eat a healthy diet when suddenly all they want is chocolate and chips?
- Should I be worried that my child is throwing themselves on the floor if I ask them to do something they don't want to do?
- What is the best way to approach potty training?
- Why won't my child go to bed?

> 'Growing up is fraught with risk and no matter what sort of parent we choose to be we will sometimes get it wrong and so will our children. Guilt is a futile emotion, but learning and doing the best we possibly can is always a possibility.'
>
> Jan Fortune-Wood, author of *Winning Parent, Winning Child.*

- How can I encourage my child to share toys with other children?

- Which type of childcare is right for my child?

- When will things improve?

These are all questions that will be addressed in this book. Before you can resolve any problem, you need to understand the underlying causes. Only then will you be able to explore possible solutions. This applies equally to parenting as it does with any other form of problem solving.

No one can tell you how to care for your child – there are many different approaches to parenting and some will fit in with your values and lifestyle and others will not. But by understanding why your child is behaving in a certain way and then exploring a range of practical strategies, you will be able to find the best way to work with your two-year-old to achieve a harmonious household.

By reading this book you will learn:

- To understand why your two-year-old is acting the way they are.

- What causes tantrums and how to avoid them.

- How to toddler-proof your home to ensure a safe environment.

- Coping strategies for when you are out and about.

- Ways to help your child get a good night's sleep.

- Some tips for getting your child to eat a balanced diet.

- How to offer your child stimulating play opportunities.

- Strategies for embarking on toilet training without tears.

- What to consider when looking for childcare.

- How to look after yourself and when to seek help.

This essential guide will provide practical strategies to guide you step-by-step through the everyday challenges of parenting during the terrible twos: from dealing with tantrums and picky eating to managing toilet training and preparing for nursery.

This book aims to arm you with essential knowledge and resources to make you and your toddler happier, enabling you to support your child through this potentially difficult phase while remaining sane!

Acknowledgements

This book is dedicated to my awesome son, Etienne, who continues to teach me much more than I will ever teach him.

I am grateful to the many people who helped me develop my thinking on the 'terrible twos', culminating in this guide. Huge thanks to all the amazing parents who so generously shared their experiences with me in person and online. To Samantha Barrett-Acquah, Dawn Colclasure-Wilson, Colette Concannon, Karen Dalgado, Elaine Hobbs, Kim, Mariam, Rachel Pattisson, Shannon, Marianne Whooley, thank you for allowing me to quote you in the guide (double thanks to Karen for helpful comments on the entire manuscript). Thanks also to sleep counsellor, Victoria Dawson.

The quotes from *How to Survive the Terrible Twos: Diary of a Mother Under Siege* are reproduced with kind permission from the author, Caroline Dunford. Special thanks are also due to Jan Fortune-Wood for making me think long and hard, and for her kind permission to reproduce the quotes from *Winning Parent, Winning Child: Parenting So That Everybody Wins.*

Finally, to Emma Gubb, Kate Gibbard and all at Need2Know, thank you for taking me and the book on!

Disclaimer

This book is written by a parent who is a qualified early years teacher. It is primarily a collection of ideas and is not intended as a substitute for individual professional advice. The author advises that she does not claim medical qualifications. Anyone with concerns about their child's physical or emotional wellbeing should consult their doctor or health visitor for individual advice.

Chapter One

Understanding the Terrible Twos

What are the terrible twos?

'Terrible twos' is a term that refers to a normal developmental stage that children go through sometime around their second to third year. It is common for children to present challenges to their parents around this time. Most people associate the terrible twos with temper tantrums, but there is much more to it than that.

Characteristics of the terrible twos

The key characteristics of this developmental stage include:

- Being in to everything.
- Saying no to everything.
- Opposing you by doing the opposite of what you ask.
- Behaving negatively towards caregivers.
- Frequent mood changes.
- Temper tantrums.

'Sometimes I feel like screaming too. I've just had another tussle with the Emperor about changing his nappy. This was complete with crying, screaming, throwing himself to the ground and banging his head off whatever was near by.'

Caroline Dunford, author of *How to Survive the Terrible Twos.*

> **Interesting fact**
>
> The terrible twos are sometimes referred to as a first adolescence because both stages are characterised by defiant, oppositional behaviour!

Why is my child behaving in this way?

Children don't just start acting up for no reason. Although having to deal with a tantrum in the supermarket may leave you tearing your hair out, it's important to understand why your child is behaving in this way and how you can best support them.

Naturally inquisitive

Two-year-olds are naturally inquisitive. They want to explore everything and find out how everything works. Unfortunately for you, this may mean that your prized ornaments find themselves being pulled off the mantelpiece and taken apart.

This is a two-year-old's way of learning. As they have limited prior experience, they have very little understanding of what is safe or potentially harmful. Equally, they do not yet understand what is deemed 'right' or 'wrong' or 'good' or 'bad' by you or by society. In other words, they are not trying to be difficult; they are simply exploring their world.

A sense of self

Around the time children turn two, they start developing their sense of self as a unique individual. The words 'I', 'me' and 'mine' will crop up regularly in their speech. Your child is beginning to discover who they are and what they like. This is the start of developing as a person in their own right.

Asserting individuality

Your child will begin to assert their own individuality by making choices. At first, this may simply be a case of saying no to you and wanting to do the opposite of what you ask. It is important to remember that this is a natural part of your child growing up. They are not trying to be awkward but merely finding out about what they can and cannot do.

Frustration

Your toddler is trying to assert their growing independence but may get easily frustrated when things don't turn out the way they want. In addition, they don't yet have the language skills to easily express themselves. As a result, a temper tantrum will often occur as your toddler's way of releasing emotion and expressing themselves in the only way that they can.

How long does it last?

This developmental stage usually begins sometime during the toddler years. Although termed the terrible twos, the actual age range for this stage will vary from child to child. Some children enter this stage by the age of one, whereas some three-year-olds (whose parents might be thinking they have been blessed) may experience a personality transplant overnight. In other words, it can start at any time.

It is difficult to pinpoint the exact time that things will start to get easier but rest assured that they definitely will! This stage usually lasts for anything between one and one and a half years. Things will improve in gradual steps and every child will be different.

You may notice that your child has stopped saying no so often but is still having tantrums, for example. Or, perhaps you will find that the tantrums start to reduce in frequency and length but meal times continue to present challenges.

'Your toddler is trying to assert their growing independence but may get easily frustrated when things don't turn out the way they want. In addition, they don't yet have the language skills to easily express themselves.'

Just as you will learn strategies to support your child, your child will learn how to make and live with decisions, and how to assert their independence without throwing themselves on the floor.

How you can help

Your role as a parent is to allow your child to explore and learn, while pre-empting and minimising negative outcomes.

It's important to remember that your child isn't being naughty or purposely difficult. Their 'challenging behaviour' is an entirely natural, and indeed necessary, process that they have to go through.

By learning more about this normal stage in your toddler's development, you can help your child to feel safe and manage their feelings and growing independence more effectively.

Some ways to help, which we will explore in more detail in the forthcoming chapters, include:

- Providing a safe toddler-proof environment for your child to play in and allowing them opportunities to explore.

- Finding things to praise regularly.

- Offering limited choices as appropriate e.g. asking 'Would you like to drink juice or water?' rather than 'What would you like to drink?'

- Establishing routines that work for you and your toddler while remaining flexible.

- Being consistent in how you respond to tantrums so that your child learns to anticipate your response and expectations and act accordingly.

Keeping your perspective

Keeping your perspective and maintaining a sense of humour throughout the difficult times can help a great deal. When things got tough in our household, I kept saying to myself that my son's apparent wilfulness was actually a sign

'Just as you will learn strategies to support your child, your child will learn how to make and live with decisions, and how to assert their independence without throwing themselves on the floor.'

of his persistence, courage and determination. These are character traits that I want him to have as an adult, so I told myself to celebrate and admire him rather than wishing for a passive, compliant child.

The terrific twos

Although many aspects of parenting during your child's second and third year can seem daunting, this can be also be a terrific time in your lives together. Try to enjoy this stage as much as you can. Your child will be starting school before you know it and, as improbable as it may seem now, you'll no doubt find yourself reminiscing over these golden years!

Accept that there will be difficult days, but remember too that there will be wonderful times. To help you through the bad times, why not write up a list of 10 positive things about life with your two-year-old? Stick it to the fridge to look at when you find yourself forgetting the good stuff!

Some amazing facts about being a parent of a two-year-old include:

- Right now, you are the centre of your child's universe.

- You get an endless supply of kisses and cuddles.

- Very soon, there will be no more nappies!

- Playing with your two-year-old is a good excuse for being very silly. You get to dress up, have fun and play with all their toys!

- Toddlers are highly entertaining and full of funny sayings.

- Toddlers' enthusiasm is infectious.

- This year, your two-year-old will learn heaps about the world around them.

- Nothing will ever compare to the love you feel for your child.

- Helping your child to develop into their own person is one of the most rewarding things you will ever do.

'Your child will be starting school before you know it and, as improbable as it may seem now, you'll no doubt find yourself reminiscing over these golden years!'

Why I wrote this guide

I hadn't really worried too much about the terrible twos when my son was a baby. But we hit a sticky patch when he was about two and a half years old and my husband and I were called into nursery to discuss our son's behaviour. Apparently, his tantrums were escalating there.

In the days leading up to the meeting, I remember us sniping at each other, casting judgement on the cause of our son's problems. My husband: 'I told you we needed to be stricter; he needs firmer boundaries.' Me: 'It's too many rules that are the problem; he needs freedom to express himself.' Both of us: 'Well, perhaps if we'd done things differently...', blah blah blah.

We were both very anxious and stressed about what we could have possibly done wrong as parents. As we sat down with our son's key worker, we worried about what she was going to say. Was he hitting other children or staff? Was he biting or spitting? Was he breaking toys or being destructive?

We were relieved to discover he wasn't doing anything like this. He was just throwing plain old-fashioned tantrums on the floor, complete with thrashing and screaming. But they were happening often and they tended to last longer than the average!

It seemed that the main instigator of the tantrums was taking turns and sharing, something our son didn't really have to worry about at home, as he didn't have any siblings. We were told that it had got to the stage that if he wanted something, he screamed so much that the other children gave in instantly. Oh dear, I thought, is my child turning into a bully?

When we got home, our son threw a packet of raisins on the floor, jumped on his toy motorbike and ran them over, squashing them all into the nice cream rug. I asked him to stop and pick up the raisins. He refused. The result? You guessed it. A full-scale tantrum. And that was just me!

Our son threw himself to the floor screaming. 'NO! Don't want to pick up. I want Mummy to play NOW!'

I thought about the meeting and the need to be clear, calm and consistent. I asked him again to pick up the raisins and then did my best to ignore the tantrum.

'Let me know when you're ready to pick them up and then we can play', I said. 'I'm going to wait until you are ready.'

After two minutes, he realised he wasn't getting anywhere, stopped, sighed, stood up and said, 'I'm ready now', and quite cheerfully picked all of his raisins up one by one and put them back into the box. He was now singing and smiling and totally transformed from the tomato headed monster of two minutes prior.

I've totally cracked it, I thought. Of course, this wasn't true. Of course, he continued to have tantrums. And we continued to worry and be far from calm and consistent.

Some nights he even had tantrums in his sleep. 'No! NO! NOOO! It's not yours! MINE! Give it back! My jelly! You drank it! Give it BACK! Take it out your mouth!' he screamed at 2am one night, thrashing around the bed with his eyes closed, fighting with an invisible jelly thief.

The fact is, the world can seem very unreasonable and scary when you are two and learning about life. And life can be pretty overwhelming and bewildering when you are the parent of a two-year-old too. You can find yourself wondering if your child's behaviour is normal and whether you are doing your best to support them.

In my quest to find answers, I spoke to many other parents, both in person and online. It was hugely reassuring to hear their stories. Some parents had no problems with tantrums but worried themselves sick about faddy eaters. For others, the potty had become an object of much fear and hatred! Sleep regularly cropped up in the conversations.

I wrote this guide to help other parents who are going through challenging times with their two-year-olds, and worrying about what they should be doing. All two-year-olds are unique and their parents are too. Different approaches work for different people. But everyone agreed it was good to share experiences and ideas.

And as for our family? Eventually, we began to learn how best to deal with our son's tantrums. We learned how to help avoid tantrums in the first place and how to support our son when his feelings were running out of control. In turn, our son began to learn how to manage his feelings and the tantrums started to reduce in frequency and severity. It didn't happen overnight and, yes, it was hard work.

Summing Up

You will undoubtedly face challenges as the parent of a two-year-old, as your child starts to develop a sense of self and assert their individuality. However, parenting during the terrible twos doesn't have to be a time of stress and tears. This is a time of huge learning opportunities for both you and your child.

Your child is learning about his or her self and the world around them. You are learning how to stay calm and in control as a parent while encouraging your child's growing independence and allowing them to make decisions. Like everything in life, parenting during the terrible twos takes practice, patience and trial and error.

And remember, the parenting skills that you develop during this time will also prove very handy when your child becomes a teenager and starts having mood swings and tantrums all over again!

Chapter Two

Your Child's Emotions, Behaviour and Needs

Extreme emotions

We often call this phase the terrible twos because dealing with children's tantrums can be hard work for parents. But it is important to remember too that it can be hard work for your two-year-old. They will be feeling pretty terrible at times. It certainly isn't fun to feel completely out of control and overwhelmed, which is what your two-year-old is experiencing when they have a tantrum.

Two-year-olds are only at the very beginning of learning how to manage their feelings, and sometimes we can expect a bit too much of them. Even as adults we get stressed out and frustrated at times, so we can't really expect our two-year-olds to be little angels all the time. What we can do is be there for them when they feel overwhelmed and gradually help them to learn how to cope with their emotions.

Black and white

Two-year-olds experience life in black and white, with love and hate. One minute they are ecstatically happy and the next they have crumpled to the floor in deep distress. At this age, it is normal for your child to experience extreme emotions. This can be very scary for them. And sometimes for you too!

Conflicting desires

Your two-year-old will often experience conflicting desires. On the one hand, they want to be able to do things themselves and show what a big boy or girl they are. On the other hand, they are not quite ready to say goodbye to being babied.

For example, your child may be reluctant to give up their dummy when you feel they should have moved past this. Perhaps they still want their bedtime milk from a bottle, despite your attempts at introducing a cup.

It is normal for your child to experience feelings of inner turbulence as they are pulled in two directions – from wanting to be Mummy and Daddy's little baby to wanting to be a big boy or girl who 'can do it myself!' This emotional turbulence can be difficult for your child to manage and is one of the reasons why they may fly off the handle so quickly.

What is a tantrum?

A tantrum can take many forms but may include some or all of the following:

- Throwing themselves on the floor and thrashing.
- Screaming.
- Spitting.
- Biting.
- Punching.
- Repeatedly saying no.

A tantrum usually takes place when a child cannot manage their feelings. This may be because they are frustrated because they cannot do something. For example, your child may be trying to build a tower and it keeps falling down, and they end up throwing themselves on the floor alongside the blocks.

Or you may have said no to something and they are angry that they cannot do what they want. This is a normal human reaction and they are not being naughty. However, this doesn't mean that you should never say no to your child. We will look at how to set limits in the next chapter. In time, your child will learn how to cope when they cannot get their own way, but right now they just don't have the emotional tools.

Although tantrums begin as a basic way of your two-year-old communicating their frustration and anger, they can sometimes develop into a pattern. How you react to a tantrum has a huge effect on the behavioural patterns your child develops.

Case study

Eryn's tantrums started just before she turned two years old. Eryn's mum, Colette, uses three strategies. First, Colette gauges the situation to assess possible causes, as she has noticed that tantrums often occur when Eryn is hungry or tired.

If Colette can tell it's because Eryn is exhausted, she takes her in her arms and comforts her and tells her it's okay. If that doesn't work, she makes a joke or does something funny to distract Eryn, who usually starts laughing.

If Eryn is banging doors, throwing things and screaming, Colette comes down to her level, looks her in the eye and tells her it's not acceptable. She always makes sure they share a hug when the tantrum has finished.

Colette stresses it is important to remain calm. She advises walking out of the room and counting to 10 if you feel your blood boiling. She has noticed that the calmer she stays, the less the tantrums occur and the quicker they end.

Colette blogs about motherhood at www.funkymammy.blogspot.com.

'In time, your child will learn how to cope when they cannot get their own way, but right now they just don't have the emotional tools.'

Wanting attention

'They only want attention' is a phrase that you will undoubtedly hear time and time again when discussing your child's behaviour during the terrible twos. Whether your child is indulging in head banging, spitting, throwing themselves on the floor or just plain old fashioned screaming, it is commonly believed that they are only acting up to get your attention and that the best way to deal with this is to ignore it.

Learning by association

It is true that young children will quickly learn the easiest way to get your attention. They learn by experience, by trying things out and seeing what happens. If every time your child makes a fuss at the shops you quickly produce a lollipop to keep them quiet, they will learn that making a fuss in the shops is a good strategy for getting sweets. You can't blame your child if this is what you are teaching them, and, yes, most of us have done it!

If, on the other hand, you ignore your child when they are making a fuss in the shops and reward them at the checkout with a treat if they have been helpful, they will quickly learn what is required to get the treat. They are simply learning what they have to do to get what they want. This is known as conditioning and is a form of behaviour training.

'For a reward system approach to work, you need to be specific and consistent.'

Interesting fact

Conditioning is a theory of associative learning developed by Russian physiologist Ivan Pavlov (1849-1936). He is most famous for his experiments using dogs. The term 'Pavlov's dog' is often used to describe someone who merely reacts to a situation rather than using critical thinking.

Reward systems

For a reward system approach to work, you need to be specific and consistent. If you tell a child that they will get a reward if they are 'good' or 'helpful', they will probably have a different idea to you of what constitutes 'good' or 'helpful'. You need to be specific in your expectations. What is it that you want them to do? Stay sitting in the trolley while you go through the aisles? Stop screaming? Help you put items in the trolley?

A common parenting tool that uses conditioning is the reward system, where a child learns that if they do X, they will receive Y. This can be as simple as 'if you eat your dinner, you will get an ice cream'. Or a complex system of star charts and stickers that they have to 'earn'. These devices are popular in TV parenting shows.

Results

Conditioning can get fast results and can be a useful tool as a parent of a young child, but it is important to be aware of its limitations. Remember that with this approach your child is only eating their dinner to get the ice cream, not necessarily because they are hungry. Or they are being quiet because they want you to buy them a toy at the checkout, not because they do not want to talk to you.

Caution

Critics of this approach argue that it suppresses children's ability to think for themselves. They are merely jumping through hoops to get the reward. As your child grows and develops their independence, you will want them to develop their own reasoning and powers of critical thinking. Like most things, it is usually a question of balance.

The importance of self-esteem

Children will naturally do anything they can to get your attention. This is because children really do need your positive attention to develop a positive self-image and self-esteem.

What is self-esteem?

We all have a particular image of ourselves. We call this a self-image. It is not fixed and may change over time. We believe certain things about ourselves, e.g. I am fat, I am clever, I am stupid, I am too loud, I am funny.

If we have a positive self-image, we are said to have high self-esteem. That is, we hold ourselves in high esteem. We think we are important, worthwhile, valued, loved human beings. If we have a largely negative self-image, the opposite may be true. If we believe that we are stupid, we may not dare try a new challenge for fear of failure. It is very important for young children to develop their self-esteem.

Where does self-esteem come from?

Your child will form a picture of themselves in a number of ways. One important way is by feeling loved and valued by their parents. This will depend on how you behave towards your child and what you say to them.

The other way a child develops self-esteem is through mastery. When they try to do something and succeed, when they master a skill (such as doing a puzzle, catching a ball, building a tower), they feel good about themselves and develop a positive self-image. This is why it is so important that your child is allowed to explore.

'Your child will form a picture of themselves in a number of ways. One important way is by feeling loved and valued by their parents. This will depend on how you behave towards your child and what you say to them.'

Your child's needs

Dr Abraham Maslow combined a large body of research to create a psychological theory called the Hierarchy of Needs, conceptualised as a pyramid (see opposite page). This hierarchy describes the stages of human development through which children must pass to become fully functioning, responsible adults, ultimately moving towards the goal of self-fulfilment.

According to the theory, a baby begins life at the bottom level and only a few adults ever reach the top. Each step is dependent on the step before it.

Your role

To help your child on their journey to the top of the pyramid, you need to ensure that their needs are met at each step. Their biological needs are fairly easy to meet. We will look further at safety in the next chapter and it goes without saying that you love your child and give them plenty of affection.

Unconditional positive regard

Children need to feel loved no matter what they do. It is important to communicate to our children that we love and accept them totally even when they do things that we do not like. This is called unconditional positive regard.

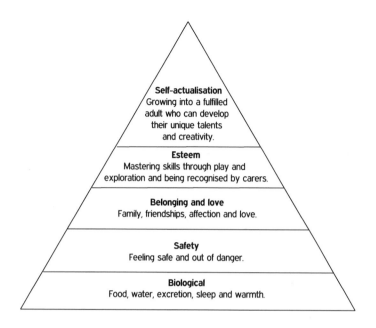

Self-actualisation
Growing into a fulfilled
adult who can develop
their unique talents
and creativity.

Esteem
Mastering skills through play and
exploration and being recognised by carers.

Belonging and love
Family, friendships, affection and love.

Safety
Feeling safe and out of danger.

Biological
Food, water, excretion, sleep and warmth.

(Hierarchy of Needs, based on Maslow, 1943.)

Interesting fact

Carl Rogers (1902-1987), an influential American psychologist who founded the humanistic approach to psychology, said that unconditional positive regard is essential for children's healthy development.

Label the behaviour not the child

What this means in practice is that we need to think about our own language and behaviour around our children. Try not to tell your child that they are naughty or bad. Explain what it is that you are not happy about, i.e. the action or behaviour. Children aged two have not developed full reasoning so will only

'My motto is a spoonful of kindness, lashings of love and an ounce of firmness. Praising your child whenever they do something good is wonderful for their confidence and wellbeing. My girl is so confident in herself and grounded, but her bossy side comes out every so often!'

Colette, mum to Eryn (aged two and a half).

partly understand why you are cross. However, they are sensitive enough to absorb and internalise negative labels, such as 'naughty boy' or 'bad girl'. Think carefully about the language you use.

On the same side

Try to maintain an atmosphere where you and your child are both 'on the same side'. It can be all too easy for parent-child relations to resemble a battle ground at times, but it doesn't have to be this way. Developing a sense of camaraderie with your child is important, so share activities and have fun together. When things do get hairy, make sure your child knows that you are listening to them and considering their feelings and needs.

Allow your child to express feelings

Always allow your child to express their feelings and don't teach them that it is 'bad' to feel angry as this can have negative consequences later on. If your child gets frustrated, give them a moment to scream, and acknowledge that they are feeling frustrated, angry or sad about whatever it is.

Allow your child to explore

In order for them to develop their self-esteem, your child needs to be able to master new skills and be recognised for doing so. Plenty of opportunities for play and exploration are needed. We will look further at this in chapter 4.

'Always allow your child to express their feelings and don't teach them that it is "bad" to feel angry as this can have negative consequences later on.'

Summing Up

Two-year-olds experience extreme emotions such as anger and frustration, which can cause them to have tantrums. Tantrums can take many forms and usually take place when a child cannot manage their feelings. It is normal for your two-year-old to get frustrated if they cannot do something and to be angry if you say no to something.

In time, they will learn how to cope with their feelings. They will also learn by observing how you react to them. You need to think carefully about what you teach your child.

Children need your love and attention to grow into fulfilled adults. It is important that they feel loved no matter what they do that may annoy you. Your child needs plenty of opportunities to explore and master new skills in order to develop their self-esteem.

Chapter Three

Freedom and Limits

Testing the boundaries

You will undoubtedly have heard people say that children need limits. 'She's just testing the boundaries.' But what exactly are boundaries and limits, and how do they apply to your two-year-old?

Have you ever had the kind of day when you've watched your two-year-old tread on the cat's tail, pull down the table cloth along with the potted plant and proceed to grind the mud into the new carpet with their ride-along truck?

A clear message

Setting limits means giving your child a clear message about lines that they mustn't cross. It is about teaching them what is and isn't acceptable. It is important to be consistent so that they can learn what is expected from them.

Why set limits?

There are several reasons why you might want to set limits. These include:

- Preventing danger.
- Balancing the whole family's needs.
- Helping your child fit in with society.

Preventing danger

Some limits are necessary to prevent danger. For example, you wouldn't allow your two-year-old to cross the road alone. You would insist on them holding your hand. You will necessarily place limits on certain activities that involve the risk of harm.

'Your two-year-old may believe that the world revolves around them, but the truth is that they do not exist in a vacuum. They are part of a family, with parents and possibly other siblings. There is nothing wrong with balancing your own needs with your child's needs.'

Balancing the whole family's needs

You may feel it is important to set some limits to balance the needs of the whole family. Your two-year-old may believe that the world revolves around them, but the truth is that they do not exist in a vacuum. They are part of a family, with parents and possibly other siblings. There is nothing wrong with balancing your own needs with your child's needs.

Helping your child fit in with society

Limits within the family also teach your child what is and what isn't considered socially acceptable behaviour in a wider context. This understanding helps your child to fit in with their peers and operate in social settings, such as playgroups and nurseries.

There are some things that you will not allow your child to do because they are not considered socially acceptable. For example, you will want your child to know that it is not acceptable to hit other children. You will teach them that we wear clothes when we go out in public – we don't go out naked.

There are some limits that everyone will agree on. We will probably all agree on teaching children that it is unacceptable to hurt others. However, other limits will be more subjective and vary from parent to parent.

Evaluating the need for limits

There can be a fine line between discouraging socially unacceptable behaviour and suppressing individuality. Always consider the reasons behind the limits that you are setting. Questions you might want to ask yourself include:

- What do you want the limit to achieve?
- How important do you rate this?
- Are there any possible drawbacks in setting this limit?
- What might happen if you don't set this limit?

The role of boundaries in relationships

Every human relationship has boundaries. A boundary is a code of conduct between two people about what is and isn't acceptable. A healthy relationship is based on mutual respect where each person can clearly express their needs and limits.

Boundaries are not absolute. They will vary from person to person. For example, some people are more touchy-feely than others. Where one person may feel fine hugging and kissing a friend, another person may feel that this invades their personal space. Boundaries will also vary on the context of the relationship. For example, acceptable behaviour between lovers will be very different from acceptable behaviour between work colleagues.

Boundaries will also vary from parent to parent. Most parents will agree that children need to understand certain boundaries – for example, that it is not okay to hit or bite people. However, all parents will have their own ideas about the scope that rules and limits play in their parenting. There is no one right way to parent, but it is important to make sure that any boundaries are fair, clearly set and age appropriate.

Positive use of boundaries

Setting boundaries in a positive way will help your child to socialise with other children. It also provides a model to help them learn how to set their own boundaries in the future.

Respecting your child's boundaries

You should also consider your child's boundaries. If they say no to something or want something to be done a certain way, their feelings and preferences deserve consideration. By respecting your child's needs and wishes as far as you possibly can, you will be offering them a positive role model.

One example where your child's boundaries are important is privacy. A two-year-old often doesn't have much of an idea about privacy. However, by the time they reach three, many children can begin to want privacy when going to the toilet. Expecting your child to let a younger child watch them on the toilet to help with their toilet training isn't necessarily reasonable.

'Bailey can understand a lot. He listens to me and then decides if he wants to trust what I'm saying and not do it. If his interest in the thing is too much, he'll just do it anyway and give me a cheeky grin.'

Karen, mum to Leo (aged three) and Bailey (aged two).

Responding to inappropriate behaviour

If your child is behaving inappropriately, such as hitting another child, there are a range of steps you can take to diffuse the situation:

- Ask your child to stop the behaviour and explain why. For example, tell your child that what they are doing is hurting someone.

- Ask your child to say sorry. Depending on their age and development, they may not fully understand the meaning of apologising yet but it is a good habit to get them into.

- If the behaviour persists, repeat the explanation and explain that if they do it again, they won't be able to play.

- If the behaviour persists, remove your child from the scene and explain why you are doing so.

- Try to prevent negative behaviour by observing your child and looking out for triggers. Does the behaviour often occur at a particular time? Perhaps they always act up when they are hungry or tired. Do problems often arise during a particular activity? Perhaps they are bored or frustrated by the activity. Try making changes accordingly and see what happens.

- Praise your child when they are behaving in ways you want to encourage. If you only notice the bad stuff, things can get pretty miserable.

- Make sure you have one-to-one time with your child every day playing together and doing fun things. Sometimes, children act up because they need your attention and don't know how else to get it.

- Read stories with your child. Your child will learn to identify with the characters and their feelings. This will help them to deal with their own feelings, as well as empathise with others.

Remember that very young children are not yet capable of reasoning fully. Avoid lengthy explanations. It can be helpful to redirect their attention to something else if they start to misbehave.

Don't be surprised if your child promises not to do something again and then goes right ahead and does it. They are not necessarily trying to be difficult. The chances are that they don't really understand yet what it is you don't want them to do or why.

Don't let this put you off trying to explain why they shouldn't kick the cat or pour their soup on the sofa. Keep your explanation simple and be prepared to repeat it many times before it sinks in or has any impact.

Parental power

Setting boundaries isn't an excuse for running your family like a military camp.

If you are always barking orders at your child, don't be surprised if your child orders other children around as soon as they get the chance. You don't want your child to turn into a bully.

'Do as I say because I say so' isn't a good model for any child. If you act like a dictator in the home, you run the risk of your child learning to become aggressive or conversely becoming passive and having no mind of their own.

Saying 'no' to 'no'

Do you ever have days when you feel that all you seem to do is say no to your child? 'Don't do that!' 'Stop touching that!' 'No!' It can become quite depressing for both parent and child when you get into a negative spiral.

'We were smacking the back of their hands as punishment for a while and then we realised that the twins were becoming quite smacky themselves. We decided to stop all hand smacking and since then they are both significantly less physical.'

Shannon, mum to Nick and Nora, twins (aged two).

Of course, sometimes it is appropriate to say no. If your child is about to put their hand in the fire or drink a bottle of bleach, you obviously need to say no, don't you? But it isn't quite as simple as that.

Obviously, the most sensible thing to do is make sure that the bleach is firmly locked out of reach in the first place. However, when children do try to do things which are potentially dangerous, it is important to think about what they are trying to get out of the experience and if there is any other way to offer them this in a safe context.

In her thought-provoking book, *Winning Parent, Winning Child*, Jan Fortune-Wood (who has four children of her own) explains how battles can be avoided and replaced with a home environment where parents and children both 'win'. She offers an example of a toddler reaching for a bottle of bleach. Jan explains that if you take the bottle of bleach away with a firm no, all the toddler experiences is refusal.

If, on the other hand, you consider what they are trying to get out of the experience, you can offer them a safe alternative. Did they like the sensation of shaking a bottle of liquid? In which case, offer them a bottle of water to shake instead. Were they drawn by the shiny label? Wrap a bit of foil around the water bottle. You get the idea.

With a bit of creativity, it is possible to avoid having to keep refusing your child experiences by offering them viable alternatives for pleasure and learning.

> 'We may only be able to use very simple words or we may need to rely on visual or practical demonstration, but we can definitely discern toddlers' preferences.'
>
> Jan Fortune-Wood, author of *Winning Parent, Winning Child.*

Case study

Karen and Adrian have two children: Leo (aged three) and Bailey (aged two).

Karen does not believe in limiting her children. She believes that everything they do is a natural part of their development, and any time we interfere/manipulate/coerce or try to control what they do, we are hindering the course of the natural development individual to that particular child.

Karen tries to let her children do whatever they want as long as it's not hurting anyone else or themselves, or damaging property. She says, 'I need to have a really good reason to actually physically stop them doing something. If it's something that I just don't really want them to do then I try to explain it to them so they can understand why.'

Karen's aim is to give her children all the information they need to make their own decisions and choices. For example, if it's cold and they want to take their coats off, she explains that she doesn't think they should because it is cold and they might get ill, but she still allows them to make their own decisions.

Toddler proofing

One way to avoid having to say no all the time is to provide a safe, toddler-proof environment for your child to play in. The first thing to do is to carry out a risk assessment of your home. Get down on the floor on your knees and walk around at toddler level to see what you can get hold of and what damage you can cause.

Potential areas to consider include:

- Stair gates.
- Keeping hazardous substances (e.g. bleach) out of reach.
- Cupboard locks.
- Loose wires.
- Plug sockets.
- Corner covers.

You can buy off the shelf childproofing safety kits (containing socket covers, childproof safety locks, etc.) which some parents may find helpful.

'At this age, the world is fascinating to your child and they may well want to stop to inspect an ant just when you want to get a move on.'

Out and about

Your child will probably be at the stage where they want to walk everywhere. This can mean that it takes two hours to get to the bus stop at the end of your road. At this age, the world is fascinating to your child and they may well want to stop to inspect an ant just when you want to get a move on.

Perhaps you have found yourself shouting at your child to hurry up – who hasn't? Or maybe they keep veering worryingly close to the kerb and you respond by barking, 'Come back!' Maybe you've experienced the heart stopping moment of your child making a dash for it and have found yourself screaming at them.

Of course, you cannot give your child complete freedom when you are out and about. But there are things you can do to help make trips as stress free as possible:

- Allow extra time.
- Check out facilities/travel before you go.
- Take a buggy for when your child gets tired.
- Consider using safety harnesses or wrist straps for walking.
- Hold hands crossing the road.

Routines

It is commonly believed that young children like routine as they can anticipate what is coming next and this helps them to feel safe. Bedtime routines can be particularly helpful. A typical bedtime routine might consist of a bath, changing into pyjamas, warm milk, brush teeth, story time, sleep. We will look more closely at this in chapter 5.

But you said...

If you let your child go to bed at 10pm most nights and then suddenly insist they must be in bed by seven because they need sleep, they won't know if they are coming or going.

If you keep changing the goal posts, it can become difficult for your child to accept what you are saying. It can be overwhelming and anxiety provoking for a young child to have no idea of parental expectations.

This doesn't mean that you should be inflexible and unresponsive to your child's needs and desires. Rather, it means that it is not a good idea to present things as rules unless you think they are sensible and you intend to stick with them.

'I try as much as possible to let them explore their own abilities and not hinder them by saying "be careful" all the time. Obviously that's easier said than done and occasionally it is necessary to use that phrase, but I try not to over use it.'

Karen, mum to Leo (aged three) and Bailey (aged two).

Balance

Like all things, balance is the key. Sensible but flexible routines for bedtimes and mealtimes can be helpful. However, insisting that your child must eat lunch at the table at 12pm religiously every day no matter what can be counter-productive. Perhaps they had a big breakfast and are just not hungry yet. Maybe it would be nice to have a picnic in the park with friends half an hour later.

Encouraging decision making

As your child develops, you want to encourage them to start making their own choices and decisions. Having too many rules, boundaries and fixed routines can sometimes get in the way of allowing a child freedom to think for themselves and exercise decision making. However, allowing your two-year-old free reign may seem like a scary prospect.

Offering limited choices

One approach is to begin by offering a limited choice. For example, rather than saying, 'What would you like to drink?' you might ask, 'Would you like juice or water?' This approach allows your child to begin exercising their own decision making within a manageable context.

If you offer an open-ended choice, you may set yourself up for disaster – for example, if your child has set their heart on drinking a chocolate milkshake right now and you don't have any. Observe and find out what they like and remember to buy it next time.

It can also be rather overwhelming for a two-year-old to suddenly be presented with too many choices, after not having many at all. This doesn't mean that you shouldn't offer choice but rather that it is introduced gradually.

Summing Up

Setting limits is about teaching your child what is and isn't acceptable behaviour. Limits can help prevent danger, balance the whole family's needs and help your child fit in with society. It is important to be consistent so that your child can learn what is expected.

Having too many rules and regimes can be counter-productive and get in the way of your child's need to explore and express themselves. Toddler-proofing the environment and engaging in creative parenting will help with this.

As your child develops, you want to encourage them to start making their own choices and decisions. An ideal starting point is offering a limited choice.

Chapter Four

Play Time

Why is play so important?

Play is your two-year-old's work. At this stage, there is simply no distinction between work and play. All activities provide opportunities for learning as well as for fun. Your two-year-old will be motivated by their curiosity and the need to seek pleasure and learning.

Play isn't just about expensive toys and organised games. Everything your child does is part of their play. Everything you do with your child can therefore facilitate their play.

Make household chores fun

Even the most mundane of household chores, such as cleaning and preparing food, can provide play opportunities for your two-year-old. Children love getting involved and helping out in grown-up activities.

It's easy to give your child a role alongside what you are doing. Let them have their own chopping board or bowl to play with while you cook. Give them a duster and let them follow you around the house while you clean.

'I set up my son's toy zoo or train set before I go to bed, so that when I come down in the morning he will be so excited to play that I can change and feed my daughter without him realising he's waiting.'

Kim, mum to two children (aged two years and five months).

Case study

Elaine, mum to Etana, aged three, demonstrates that play activities don't have to involve expensive toys. When Etana was two, Elaine started introducing nature collages. She would take Etana to the park to collect leaves and twigs, and then go home and stick them onto paper. Etana loved it!

Elaine also swears by play dough, as it gets the imagination going and has endless possibilities. She found it a real life saver when taking two-year-old Etana on a nine hour flight.

Dressing up is another family favourite. Elaine says her scarves become princess saris and her boots, glass slippers! You can combine sticking, play dough and dressing up to make crowns and masks to wear, and pretend the park is a jungle!

These were all activities that Elaine enjoyed doing with her daughter, which can make all the difference. If you are having fun, so will they. Elaine's top tip is not to worry about the mess until afterwards, as children can pick up on your anxiety and hold back.

Play is learning

When your child is playing in the bath, watching their duck float or filling and emptying containers, they are actually learning scientific and mathematical concepts. They are asking themselves questions and testing hypotheses. Will it float? Will it sink? How much water can I fit in there? Which container holds more? Ah, I think it's the red one. Let's see. Oh no, it's not, it's the green!

Learning through play covers all areas of children's development, including their language development, literacy, problem-solving skills, motor skills and emotional and social skills. We will look at each of these in turn shortly.

Educational toys

These days, there are many high-tech so-called educational toys on the market that claim to teach your child particular skills, such as problem solving, language development or motor skills. These include DVDs, videos and flashcards. Your child does not need these special resources to learn.

According to *The Trouble with 21st Century Kids* complied by Peter Smith and Rachel Biggins, some researchers believe that over-use of pre-programmed electronic toys and other games with rules encourages a child to be motivated by the outcome rather than the process of playing. In turn, it is believed that this can stifle children's creativity and imagination.

In her book, *Einstein Never Used Flash Cards,* American child development expert Professor Kathy Hirsh-Pasek warns that so-called 'smart' toys and videos can also hinder social skills. She recommends the use of traditional building blocks, play dough, crayons, costumes, paints and balls. These help children learn how to play imaginatively and develop key skills such as problem solving and perseverance.

There is nothing wrong with allowing your child to play with high-tech electronic toys if they enjoy them, but balance is key. Make sure they get lots of variety in their play opportunities, including experimental play when your child is trying things out to see how they respond. Children can learn as much, if not more, from playing with everyday household objects and simple toys.

Television

Many people also have strong feelings about young children watching television. Everyone would agree that sitting your child in front of the television all day is not a good idea. But allowing your child to sing along to their favourite programme on CBeebies isn't going to hurt them, as long as it isn't all they ever do.

Watching television can be harmful if it is at the expense of engaging in creative and social play. Like everything else, balance is key. There is no need to feel guilty for letting your child watch their favourite programme while you get on with dinner or simply have a cuppa. And always remember that if you ban something, it can instantly become much more appealing. In reality, not many two-year-olds would actually want to sit and watch television all day anyway.

'Francesca loves playing in her "tent", made by draping a big blanket over two chairs. She has all her toys in there and pretends she is keeping dry, out of the rain! She wants every visitor we have to come and play in there!'

Rachel, mum to Francesca (aged two and a half) and Elizabeth (aged 10 months).

Adult directed play vs child directed play

With adult directed play, you are taking the lead in setting up an activity for your child. This can either be a game, toy or a household activity. There are some activities that your child cannot do completely by themselves, such as baking a cake.

Have you ever seen your child pretending that the sofa is a boat or the dining chairs are a train? Perhaps they play under the table in their secret castle? This is called child directed play or free-flow play, where the child initiates the activity themselves. This is when their imagination really kicks in.

You can encourage your child to initiate play by offering them a range of play opportunities. Most young children love dressing up and making dens. Old clothes and accessories, fabric, boxes and containers can provide endless opportunities.

Sometimes, your child will want to play alone. At other times, they might want a play companion. Try to join in with your child's self-initiated activity without taking over. Ask them what they are doing and whether they would like you to play. Young children love making up the rules for their parents.

'Etana's favourite things to do are sticking, play dough and dressing up. Luckily all things you can do on a budget!'

Elaine, mum to Etana (aged three).

Making up their own games

You might notice that your child plays with a toy in a different way than it was intended. Perhaps you have given your child some small musical instruments to play and you are dismayed to find them rolling the drum off the end of the sofa. Don't be! They are engaged in all-important experimentation and learning about balance and gravity.

It is important not to correct them and tell them that there is a right way to play with the toy. Young children develop their creativity when left to make up their own games.

Focus on process not product

It is important not to always focus on the end product of an activity, such as building the perfect tower or making a beautifully iced cake. As a parent, it is easy to fall into this trap. We have all had days where we 'help' our child create a fantastic looking painting or junk model, only to realise later on that we did most of it ourselves while our child watched!

At this stage, the process is infinitely more important than the product. Don't set goals or start an activity with a preconceived outcome. Allow your child to take the lead. Let your child get stuck in and get their hands dirty. Don't worry if the biscuits don't look great or the model dog has five legs. Your child will love working imaginatively and creating things of their own. Your role is to facilitate this.

At the same time, remember to celebrate their 'work' by displaying their models and paintings around the house. Just because their picture looks like a scribble to the adult eye, it doesn't mean it should be treated as rubbish and chucked away. When your child sees that you are valuing their creations, it helps them to value themselves.

Emotional and social skills

Your two-year-old is only just beginning to develop the social skills needed to be able to share toys and take turns with their friends. One way of helping your child in this area is to model sharing and turn-taking behaviour with your child.

You can do this with simple play activities, such as building a tower together: 'Now it is my turn to add a block, now it is your turn'. Your child will copy this behaviour when they play with other children.

Role play

Role play activities using dolls, soft toys and puppets can offer your child the opportunity to act out different roles and feelings. This can help your child express their emotions and needs. Young children will often use toys in this way: for example, saying, 'teddy tired' or 'dolly sad'.

'Francesca is good at drawing a noughts and crosses board and can draw noughts and take turns playing. The rules are very loosely applied. She enjoys it never the less.'

Rachel, mum to Francesca (aged two and a half) and Elizabeth (aged 10 months).

This is something you can play with your child. For example, you could put on the voice of one toy and engage in a conversation with your child's toy. Imaginative role play can be encouraged through the provision of dolls and dolls' houses, home corners, construction toys and small world play environments, such as play hospitals, farms, shops, etc.

If you observe your child playing with these types of toys, you will often see how they initiate conversations and re-enact things they have seen in everyday life and on television. It is important to allow your child to play alone at times. However, you can also help extend their play by asking questions about what they are doing and acting in role with them.

Rough and tumble play

Two-year-olds enjoy engaging in physical play with their peers, as well as adults. Rough and tumble play includes climbing, running, chasing, play fighting, kicking and throwing. It is important not to restrict your child from engaging in this type of play with peers at the local playground or when friends come round.

Research by Tannock, Lyons and Sileo, from the University of Nevada, shows that although rough and tumble play mimics intentionally aggressive action, it is merely symbolic and not intended to hurt others. Rough and tumble play allows your child the opportunity to develop key social skills, such as co-operation, conflict resolution, turn taking, leadership skill development and control of impulses.

Language development

As well as helping your child develop emotional and social skills, play also stimulates language development as your child will be engaged in speaking and listening. The role play activities discussed in the previous section are particularly helpful here.

'Francesca loves taking her "baby" for walks round the house in the toy pushchair. This also makes for quite speedy walks to the shops in real life too!'

Rachel, mum to Francesca (aged two and a half) and Elizabeth (aged 10 months).

At two years old, your child will probably be saying quite a few words and phrases now. Some will be talking more than others. Young children communicate non-verbally too by facial expressions, body language and pointing. Like all areas of child development, every child is different and progresses at their own rate.

You can help stimulate your child's language development by spending time interacting and talking with them as much as you can.

Story time

Sharing stories together is another important activity. Your child will enjoy sitting with you and reading a book. As you read, point to the words and encourage your child to point to the words so they start to get the idea that the words on the page relate to the words you are saying aloud. You can both point to the pictures too.

Ask questions as you go along, e.g. 'What do you think the farmer is doing?', 'Can you see where the caterpillar has gone?' This will help to engage your child fully in the story and help them to think about what is happening.

Young children often have favourite books that they like to read over and over again. They enjoy the anticipation of knowing what comes next. You may find that your child is able to remember the exact words on the page. But be careful not to make reading a chore by labouring over the words. Always go at your child's pace.

Try not to worry too much about teaching them to read at this stage. Igniting their passions for stories is the most important thing for now. Make it fun. Consider dressing up in character or using toys and puppets to act out the story. You can incorporate the stories into other forms of play such as mask making and other crafts relating to the story.

Stories can also help your child with their emotional and social skills as they relate to the characters.

Problem solving

When your child is engaged in creative, imaginative play, they are naturally engaged in problem solving. 'What happens if I put that there?', 'How can I get this to fit on there?'

Young children can bore of expensive toys when there are limited ways to play with them. The two-year-old's world is exploring and experimenting to find out how things behave and respond.

Motor skills

Gross motor skills include crawling and walking, whereas fine motor skills include hand-eye co-ordination, mark-making and drawing. These are developed naturally by engaging in a wide range of play, including arts and crafts as well as physical play.

Outdoor play

Outdoor play gives children the opportunity to explore with their whole body, engaging all their senses. Outdoor play can happen anywhere outdoors: your garden, the local park, an adventure playground, a trip to the beach. You don't have to travel far. If you have a garden, consider setting up a sand pit and a paddling pool in good weather.

Local facilities

You can get information on local play facilities from your health visitor. They will be able to tell you about children's centres and local parent and toddler groups.

It is also worth checking out your local library as many hold regular toddler story time sessions. Many also offer craft sessions, such as mask making and model making, often to fit in with topics, seasons or festivals.

Summing Up

Your two-year-old will enjoy a wide range of play activities. Play provides rich opportunities for learning in all areas of children's development, including their language development, literacy, problem-solving skills, motor skills and emotional and social skills.

Play isn't just about expensive toys and organised games. Play is also about everyday activities, talking and interacting. It is important to get a balance between adult-directed and child-directed play. At this age, the focus of play should be on the process not the end product.

Chapter Five

⌣ ⌣Sleep

...otive and challenging for parents of young ...getting enough? What about you? Is your ...ey started waking in the night? What can you ...o for everyone in the household?

in *The No-Cry Sleep Solution for Toddlers and* ...en under the age of five do not sleep through

...gh?

...n their sleep needs. The majority of two-year-olds seem to need be...... and 12 hours of sleep a night. If your child still has a good daytime nap, they may need less sleep at night.

Bedtimes

Bedtimes can vary enormously and, like everything else, there is no wrong or right way. A common bedtime for a two-year-old seems to be between 7.30pm and 8.30pm. Your child may go to bed as early as 7pm. However, if your child is napping during the day or simply doesn't need as much sleep as the average two-year-old, a considerably later bedtime is not inappropriate.

You can't (and shouldn't try to) force a child to go to bed and sleep if they are not tired. However, be aware that sometimes children will fight against bedtimes for reasons other than not being tired.

> 'Sleep issues are never ending. As for strategies, I usually ask friends what worked for them. I also googled a sleep clinic for advice, as sometimes I cannot figure out what is upsetting the routine.'
>
> Elaine, mum to Etana (aged three).

Resisting bedtime and night waking

There can be a variety of reasons for your two-year-old resisting bedtime or waking in the night.

Separation anxiety

Perhaps you had a baby who settled down to sleep perfectly well alone, but is now appearing fearful at bedtime or upon waking in the night. This is not at all unusual. It is common for a two-year-old to experience separation anxiety and be fearful of being alone without Mummy or Daddy.

During the terrible twos, your child is beginning to understand that they are an individual who is separate from you. It is exciting for your child to realise that they are their own person. But it can be frightening too.

Fertile imaginations can conjure up a variety of fears – from green hairy monsters under the bed, to spiky wolves at the window and spiders on the ceiling. Your child may need reassurance that there are no monsters in the room, which might involve checking under the bed.

Your child may feel more comfortable with a night light kept on, and/or the bedroom door left ajar. Some children may only feel relaxed enough to fall asleep with a parent in the room or with physical contact – either lying next to them or holding their hand.

How you respond to this is very much down to your personal choice. Many parents are happy to stay with their child until they have fallen asleep. However, others do not feel this is practical or desirable. Your take on this issue, as with all areas of parenting, will depend on your values, beliefs and lifestyle.

Over stimulation

Another reason for wakefulness at bedtime is over stimulation. As adults, we usually need some wind down time before going to bed, perhaps by having a relaxing bath, reading our favourite novel in bed or listening to music.

Have you ever gone to bed straight after engaging in stimulating activity and then experienced the feeling that your brain just won't shut down? I have to set myself a cut-off time in the evenings after which I must stop working. Otherwise, I find myself lying awake in my bed for ages, unable to switch off.

The same applies to children. You can't expect your child to be fully switched on one minute and then relaxed and ready to sleep the next. This is why a sensible bedtime routine is important.

Bedtime routines

A relaxing night time routine can assist greatly in establishing a peaceful bedtime, which is conducive to sleep. A typical bedtime routine might consist of having a warm bath, changing into pyjamas or a nightdress, having a drink of warm milk, brushing teeth, reading a story together and then going to sleep.

Going to bed at around the same time each night can help your child establish a regular sleep pattern, anticipate what is coming next and wind down for sleep.

'It's only now, at two and a half years old, she has a good routine. It's taken me this long to realise that I was the one that didn't want the routine.'

Colette, mum to Eryn (aged two and a half).

Case study

Colette's husband walked out on her when she was pregnant and she had to uproot and move to Ireland. Her daughter, Eryn, was a colicky baby who cried a lot, and Colette found new motherhood stressful. Colette found it easiest to have her daughter sleep in bed with her.

They have now developed a routine where Colette puts Eryn to bed at 8pm every night. Eryn sleeps in her own bed until around 2am and then goes into Colette's bed, where they sleep until 8am.

Colette is starting to encourage her daughter to stay in her own bed but says that she doesn't mind her coming in to cuddle up. The important thing for Colette is to have her daughter in bed by 8pm so she can have a break in the evenings.

Where to sleep

Your two-year-old may sleep alone in their own room, in a room with a sibling or in the same room as you. They may sleep in a cot, a cot-bed, junior bed or single bed, or they may share your bed. Many factors will influence your decision, including space, finances, your child's sleep patterns and needs, and your parenting philosophy.

Cots and beds

'Changing her from a cot to a big girl bed was fairly easy. She was asking for it for ages. She's always had her own bed, since the day we came home from hospital.'

Elaine, mum to Etana (aged three).

If your child is still sleeping in a cot, now is a good time for them to graduate to a bed. This is because a two-year-old can climb over the bars of a cot and risk falling down and hurting themselves.

Many cot-beds and junior beds have low in-built side rails to prevent your child from rolling out onto the floor. You can buy low, flexible safety bed rails to fit a single bed. These can be removed when they are no longer needed.

Many children will enjoy getting their first proper bed, as they feel it is all part of becoming a big girl or boy. You could involve them in choosing a design and setting up their new bed.

Co-sleeping

Some parents opt for co-sleeping from birth as a planned parenting choice. Co-sleeping – also known as the family bed approach – is a key part of some parenting philosophies, such as 'attachment parenting'. For more information, see www.attachmentparenting.org.

In Western society, we put a lot of value on independence. This can put pressure on parents to feel that they are not doing things right if their child is not sleeping alone. However, in many other cultures, it is usual practice for babies and young children to sleep with their parents.

As planned co-sleeping is a minority practice in Western society, if you do choose to co-sleep, you may find that you come up with some resistance from other people. Remember that if you and your child are happy and getting enough sleep, it really is nobody else's business.

Partial co-sleeping

Partial co-sleeping, when a child starts the night in their own bed and moves into the parents' bed some time during the night, often happens by default, as we saw with Colette's case study. Rather than being a planned strategy, many parents will go with the flow to accommodate their child's needs during this time.

Having informally surveyed many parents, in person and online, I would say that partial co-sleeping is more common than we might first believe. Many parents are happy to be flexible in this way, with the long-term goal of their child eventually feeling comfortable enough to sleep by themselves.

Partial co-sleeping can take many forms. Instead of your child coming into your bed, you may join your child in their bed when they wake. The advantage of this approach is that you can choose whether to stay for the whole night or just a short while. You can also alternate with your partner. The downside is that you may end up feeling like a yo-yo, popping in and out of bedrooms, especially if you have more than one child.

No right or wrong way

All families are different and this includes children, as well as parents. Some toddlers love nothing better than getting into bed with Mummy and Daddy. However, other young children enjoy having their own space and prefer to sleep in their own bed. Some parents are happy to have their two-year-old snuggling up, but others do not consider this an option.

If you only take away one thing from this book, I hope it will be to always do what feels right for your family. There is no one right way to do it.

Strategies for change

If you have come to a stage where you would like to encourage your child to stay in their own bed, there are various strategies that you can try to help bring about change. Change can be difficult for everyone, parents and children alike, so it is important to prepare carefully. If you have a partner, make sure you discuss things fully first, before you introduce changes with your two-year-old.

'We love sleeping together. Waking up next to their little faces is one of the best things in the world. We would never force them out however old they got. I'm pretty sure they're not going to want to share a bed with their mum and dad when they're 15!'

Karen, mum to Bailey (aged two) and Leo (aged three).

Talk to your child about sleep

If you have decided that you no longer want your toddler creeping into your bed at night, start by talking to them in the daytime about what happens at night.

If your own sleep is being interrupted, you could be honest with your child and tell them that you cannot sleep properly when they come in and that it makes you feel grumpy the next day. Depending on the age of your child, it may be difficult for them to take this in.

Very young children cannot fully empathise with parents' needs, but it is a good idea to let them know that you are a person with needs too. In time, they will start to understand. Talk to them about how you could do things differently. They may even suggest solutions.

One step at a time

Some parents find that an interim step of allowing their child to come and sleep in their room, without sleeping in their bed, can help. For example, you could set up another bed area or mattress in your room and explain to your child that if they wake during the night, they can come and sleep in there but they mustn't disturb you.

Once they have got used to this first change, you can think about introducing a later change to move them out of the room altogether. Once they are comfortable with sleeping without your physical contact, it will be easier to make that final step.

Being clear and consistent

Prepare your child by talking about how they will soon be sleeping all by themselves for the whole night. Be positive and upbeat – introduce the change as something exciting. This can be a good time to redecorate their bedroom or let them choose a new cuddly toy as a special sleep companion.

'If it took a hundred times of getting up and putting him back into bed, then we did it a hundred times. We had to remain calm no matter how tired we were or how long it took to get him to go to sleep. But we stuck to it and it's worked out so far.'

Dawn, mum to Jennifer (aged eight) and Jesse (aged two).

Decide on when you are going to start making changes, be clear on your approach in advance, explain to your child what will happen and stick to it. Once you have decided that you want your child to stay in their own room, explain to them in advance that if they come into your room, you will return them to their own bed every time they come in.

When they do come in, speak quietly and calmly, saying something like, 'Back to bed now', and take them back to their bed and leave the room. You may have to repeat this process many times before they finally stop coming in. Be prepared to get reduced sleep while you are going through this process.

Give your child lots of praise along the way. Focus on the positive rather than the negative. For example, say, 'Mummy and Daddy are so pleased that you only came into our room once last night and that you went straight back to your bed like a big boy' rather than, 'We told you to stay in your own bed and you still came into our room! It's not good enough!'

Dropping the daytime nap

If your child is still sleeping in the day, the thought of them dropping their daytime nap may be filling you with dread! Nap time is often the time that hard pressed mums and dads get a few chores done or find a few moments for themselves.

The advantage of your child dropping the daytime nap means that you often have more flexibility with daytime plans. It is likely that your child will go to bed earlier at night too, which can be an added bonus if you long for a bit of time to yourself in the evening.

When is the right time to drop the nap?

There is no 'right' time for your child to drop their day nap and you should always be led by your child. If your child has erratic nap times and simply falls asleep in the buggy or sofa when they are tired, you may notice that they stop falling asleep so often in the day.

'I try to tackle these problems over a weekend or holidays, so if we're tired the next day, it doesn't matter.'

Elaine, mum to Etana (aged three).

If, on the other hand, your child has a regular nap time and will only go down for a nap in their bed and with a particular routine, then you will have more parental involvement in facilitating the drop. It may be that your child stops appearing tired at their nap time and things evolve naturally.

Supporting your child to make a change

However, parents do need to closely observe and support children in making changes. Quite often, you will find that your child wants to nap later and later in the day. What starts out as an early afternoon nap straight after lunch, may slip into a 2.30pm to 3.30pm nap, and then a 4pm to 5pm nap.

The later the naps gets, the harder it can be for your child to wake up and carry on with their normal daily activities, as they may still feel tired towards the end of the day.

For example, if your child usually goes to bed at 7pm and nap time slips to 5pm, they may not readily wake up and instead start settling into a deeper sleep. You are then left with a difficult decision as to whether to wake them up and suffer a very grisly tired child who screams for bed, or let them go to bed at 5pm and risk them waking at 3am bright and eager to start their day!

Sometimes, while going through a transition process, it can help to try diversion tactics to prevent your child from falling asleep very late in the day. This can mean avoiding being out with them in the buggy or in the car seat, which often lull toddlers to sleep. It might also mean refraining from activities that tire them for a short period, while your child gets used to making it through the day without a sleep.

It is important to remain flexible and responsive to your child's needs after they have dropped their nap. If they are ill or under the weather or have simply had a very busy and tiring day or week, they may need a little daytime sleep now and then.

'It is helpful to develop a good bedtime routine. Activities that require hand-eye co-ordination, such as threading, colouring or jigsaws, are ideal in the run up to bedtime.'

Victoria Dawson, sleep counsellor.

Summing Up

Two-year-olds vary greatly but most need around 10 to 12 hours sleep a night. It is common for children to drop their daytime nap during this year, which can result in an earlier bedtime.

It is not uncommon for two-year-olds to start resisting bedtime or waking in the night. Avoiding over-stimulation before bedtime and introducing a relaxing night time routine can go a long way to helping your child settle.

How you deal with night waking will depend on your parenting philosophy and lifestyle. It is important to remember there is no one right way to do things.

Chapter Six

Meal Times

Nutrition

Most parents worry from time to time about what their children are eating. We all want to give our children a healthy, balanced diet. But it can be tricky to coax healthy food down a two-year-old at times.

My own son was a great eater when he was a baby. He took to weaning brilliantly and was eating a wide range of pureed fruit and vegetables by six months. I was thrilled not to have a picky eater to worry about, relieved that my baby wasn't going to grow up detesting his five a day.

Of course, when he turned two he wiped the smug little smile right off my face by deciding that the only things in the world worth eating were pasta, cheese and chocolate. It was a bit of a shock to me, after he had happily eaten a varied diet up until this point. However, it is not uncommon for children to become fussy eaters around the time of the terrible twos.

Toddlers' dietary needs

Your toddler needs a varied diet, just as you do. In fact, your child can eat more or less the same diet as you, give or take a few modifications. It's easier for you too if you encourage your child to eat the same food as you. It won't necessarily work all the time, as children have their own preferences and tastes, just as adults do. But it's a good starting point.

Bear in mind that you are a role model for your child. If you don't want them to eat crisps and chocolate, try to avoid eating these foods in front of them. If they see you constantly eating junk food, they will learn that this is acceptable. It's

'My single greatest priority for my children is that every second of every minute of every day, they know that they are loved. If very occasionally that love is accompanied with a side of fries, then I think that's okay.'

Shannon, mum to Nick and Nora, twins (aged two).

okay for you and your child to have treats now and then. But it isn't really fair to sit there munching through a bar of chocolate while insisting your child snacks on a celery stick.

Generally speaking, it is best to offer home-cooked foods wherever possible, rather than relying on prepared ready meals. It can be difficult to know exactly what has gone into ready meals and they can be high in salt, sugar, additives and saturated fat.

This doesn't mean that you have to be a slave to the kitchen or that you can't cut corners at all. After all, we don't all have hours to spare cooking up culinary delights three times a day. Cooking several batches of one meal in advance and freezing portions to eat at a later date can help you save time.

Not all prepared foods are bad. Frozen vegetables are usually just as nutritious as fresh ones. In fact, a frozen carrot can contain more vitamins than one that has been knocking about in the vegetable rack for a while.

Two-year-olds are usually still drinking a reasonably high intake of milk, but should also be offered water and fruit juice, which you might want to dilute first.

Food groups

A balanced diet means a good balance of protein, carbohydrate, fats, vitamins and minerals. You don't need to ban any foods altogether, but rather you should make sure you offer your child a variety of foods from each food group in the right proportions.

Fruit and vegetables can include fresh, frozen, dried and canned. Good carbohydrates include bread, rice, potatoes, cereals and pasta. Try to restrict cakes and biscuits, although it is not necessary to omit them altogether.

Milk and dairy foods, such as cheese and yoghurt, are usually popular with young children. Young children with a dairy intolerance can also be given non-dairy alternatives such as goat's milk or soya products.

Protein rich foods are important for growth. They include meat, fish, eggs, as well as vegetarian sources, such as beans and other pulses.

Although you should restrict the amount of food containing a high level of sugar and fat, it is important to remember that children do need to eat some

'I try not to worry how much Francesca eats but she always sits at the table with us at meal times and is given proper food. If she hasn't eaten much of a meal, she'll snack on a banana, some bread or yoghurt later on.'

Rachel, mum to Francesca (aged two and a half) and Elizabeth (aged 10 months).

The eatwell plate

Use the eatwell plate to help you get the balance right. It shows how much of what you eat should come from each food group.

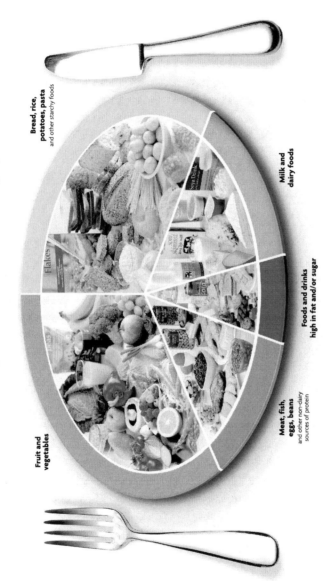

Bread, rice, potatoes, pasta and other starchy foods

Milk and dairy foods

Foods and drinks high in fat and/or sugar

Meat, fish, eggs, beans and other non-dairy sources of protein

Fruit and vegetables

fat. Fat helps the body absorb some vitamins, is a good source of energy and provides essential fatty acids that the body can't make itself.

Foods to avoid

It's generally best to avoid giving your two-year-old whole nuts, and anything that could get stuck in the throat and cause choking. If offering fruit with stones or pips, remove them before giving the fruit. You should also restrict your child's intake of salt.

Try not to give your child too many sugary treats. This doesn't mean that you should never allow them sweets. This is a matter for parental choice, but a few sweet treats now and then won't harm your child.

How much is enough?

Your child will need to chomp through a lot of calories in a day to cater for their growth. However, remember that two-year-olds only have small stomachs, so eating little and often is key. Offer your child breakfast, lunch and dinner with a mid-morning and mid-afternoon snack, and possibly a further snack before bedtime.

Try to make snacks, as well as main meals, nutritious. Slices of fresh fruit make an ideal snack, as does a small yoghurt or cubes of cheese. Young children can often still be convinced that an oat cake is a biscuit.

Your child's food intake may well go up and down from day to day and week to week. Children generally need a higher intake when they are going through a growth spurt or entering a particularly active period. They will have times when they don't need to eat so much. Children know what they need instinctively. Humans, like other mammals, are designed to eat when they are hungry. Never force your child to eat when they are not hungry or deny them food when they are.

'Bessie won't have cherry tomatoes but Alice loves them. Alice occasionally refuses carrots and then will have them another day as if she's forgotten she doesn't like them!'

Marianne, mum to Bessie and Alice, twins (aged 21 months).

Coping with picky eaters

Food fads are quite common during this time. Your child may suddenly go off food that they have always loved and eaten quite happily. Just as your child is asserting their independence and starting to make their own choices in other areas of their lives, so this will be apparent in their eating habits. They are realising that they are an individual and that they have likes and dislikes that don't always match up to yours.

Fads are not just restricted to taste but also to the appearance and presentation of food. Your child may decide that they will only eat a sandwich off their green plate and a cooked meal off their orange plate. Although this may appear irrational, remember that even as adults we all have our little rituals. If it isn't causing anyone any problems, it's generally best to go with the flow.

It is usually counter-productive to get over anxious about young children's eating habits. They will pick up on your anxiety and may even try to provoke a reaction by refusing food. Continue to offer a variety of food and don't make a big fuss if your child refuses something.

If your child is going through a picky stage, you might find it makes sense to offer simple, easy to prepare foods. If you go to a lot of trouble preparing elaborate meals in the hope of coaxing your child into trying new foods, it can be disappointing if they then turn their nose up at your efforts! Try not to take it personally.

Try to make mealtimes as fun and stress-free as possible. Find a few foods from each food group that your child likes, and then offer changes every now and then. As long as your child is eating a reasonably balanced diet, there is no need to worry.

If your child is eating a very restricted diet and excluding whole food groups for a prolonged time, or appears to be under or overweight, speak to your GP or health visitor.

'I accept when she says she doesn't want something, so long as she's tried it first. Often, she has one tiny bite and admits she likes it after all, despite previous protestations of disgust.'

Rachel, mum to Francesca (aged two and a half) and Elizabeth (aged 10 months).

Case study

Marianne has twin girls, Bessie and Alice, who are not quite two years old.

The girls can change their eating habits quite unexpectedly. They used to eat Weetabix or porridge with mashed banana, blueberries or a drop of honey for breakfast every day. One day out of the blue, they refused to touch it and now prefer dry Cheerios with raisins followed by toast and jam.

Marianne always makes a habit of re-presenting foods that were initially discarded, as she has found that the twins may try them again at a later date. Marianne offers a varied diet to her daughters. If they don't like something, Marianne will try offering an alternative. For example, they didn't like clementines but are happy to eat tinned mandarins in grape juice.

The girls eat their meals at roughly the same time each day and Marianne believes that this rhythm helps give them a sense of time. Marianne found that the girls got bored and started leaving the table if left on their own for too long. To overcome this, she brings all the food to the table at the same time, so there are no long breaks waiting for Mummy to bring in the toast!

Offering limited choices

You may wish to offer your child a limited choice of food at mealtimes. For example, you could set out some finger foods and ingredients for sandwich making and involve your child in putting their lunch together. You can ask whether they want cheese or hummus in their sandwich, whether they want chopped apple or pear.

This way, your child will feel that their preferences are being respected rather than food choices being forced on them. Be wary of offering an open choice though. If you simply ask your child what they want, 9 out of 10 times they'll ask for something you haven't got! Too much choice can also be overwhelming for a two-year-old.

Having fun with foods

Your child loves playing and using their imagination, and meal times are no exception. Involving your child in food preparation can be great fun and helps them to look forward to meal times. Many children love making dough for pizza or helping toss the salad.

Let your child make a face or pattern with pizza toppings or sandwich fillings. Try using different shaped cutters for sandwiches, not just biscuits. Let your child twist up cheese straws and make them into snakes.

Don't worry about things getting messy. Put an apron on your child and roll up their sleeves and then simply tidy up together afterwards.

Practicalities

At two, your child may have outgrown their high chair and want to join in with the rest of the family at the table. Some brands of high chairs adapt as your child gets bigger. You may be able to take the tray off so the chair can pull up to the main table. Others can be taken apart and reassembled as a small table and chair. These transforming high chairs are usually more expensive than the standard chairs but may work out to be cost effective in the long term.

Alternatively, there are various booster seats on the market which strap onto your standard dining chair to raise your child to the correct level for the table.

Two-year-olds usually enjoy feeding themselves, although sometimes they may prefer to be fed by you. This is all part of the inner conflict that two-year-olds experience as they are pulled between wanting to be 'all grown up' and not wanting to let go of being 'babied'.

You can encourage your child to feed themselves, but try not to make too much fuss if they resist at times. Most foods can be eaten with a spoon and fork but it is fine to introduce a child's (blunt) knife. They may enjoy using the knife to spread fillings on sandwiches and crackers.

'I was getting fed up of the high chairs, so I bought a small table and chairs for the twins. They loved it! Now we have booster chairs at the dining table for family meals and a small table for their breakfast.'

Marianne, mum to Bessie and Alice, twins (aged 21 months).

Summing Up

It is not uncommon for children to become fussy eaters around the time of the terrible twos. It's all part of them asserting their independence and finding out what they like and dislike.

Your two-year-old needs a varied diet and can eat more or less the same diet as you, but don't worry if they refuse certain foods. Offer them simple, easy to prepare foods and try to involve them in the process of putting a meal together. Make meal times as fun and stress free as you can.

Try not to make a fuss if your child exhibits food fads during this time. It's very common and perfectly natural for them to do so. And like every other aspect of the terrible twos, it will eventually pass.

For more specific information on children's nutrition, see *Children's Nutrition – A Parent's Guide* (Need2Know).

Chapter Seven

Toilet Training Without Tears

Is your child ready?

It is common to start potty training around the time your child turns two, but there really is no magic time to start. It very much depends on your child's physical and psychological readiness. Some children may be ready from as young as 15 months, whereas others will not be ready until after they turn three.

In some ways, the terms 'toilet training' and 'potty training' can be misleading, as you cannot train a child who is not ready or willing to co-operate in the process. Your role is to help support your child as they begin the process of gaining control over their bladder and bowel movements.

Physical readiness

A baby's bladder is physically unable to hold urine for very long and will automatically empty itself regularly. Until the bladder has developed sufficiently to hold urine for any length of time, there is no point in beginning potty training, as your child will be unable to control when they wee.

Similarly, a baby's bowel movements are controlled by an automatic reflex. Until the bowel muscles have developed sufficiently to hold faeces for any length of time, your child will be unable to control when they have a poo.

'I know some mums are adamant to get them trained at a certain age. But my own mum's advice always sticks in my head – if you are stressed, they will be stressed – so chill!'

Colette, mum to Eryn (aged two and a half).

In order to develop full bladder and bowel control, your child needs more than just strong bladder and bowel muscles. The brain needs to be able to acknowledge the need to pass faeces or urine and then send a message to the bladder or bowel. It can take time for your child to make these connections. Readiness cannot be forced.

Interesting fact

According to Dr Miriam Stoppard in *New Babycare*, about 90% of girls and 75% of boys can go without a nappy during the day by the age of two and a half.

It can take boys longer than girls to learn. Most boys learn to wee sitting down at first before they master the art of standing up.

Psychological readiness

'As well as being physically ready, your child also needs to be psychologically ready to start graduating to the potty or toilet. This means that they have to want to co-operate in the process.'

As well as being physically ready, your child also needs to be psychologically ready to start graduating to the potty or toilet. This means that they have to want to co-operate in the process. If your child feels pressurised, they are likely to refuse to co-operate. This can lead to tantrums and tears, which can make the process very difficult for your child and for you.

Dangers of starting too soon

If you start trying to introduce the potty before your child is ready, it can lead to disappointment and upset all round. Although it might not always feel like the case, your child naturally desires to please you. When they know that you want them to use the potty but they just can't manage it, they are likely to get upset and may feel guilty and ashamed. These negative feelings can then turn to resentment and anger towards you.

It is important to go gently and never to force your child to sit on a potty or toilet. Be prepared for the inevitable accidents along the way and always respond sympathetically. Never tell your child off for not wanting to sit on the potty or for having an accident.

If you misjudge the situation and discover that your child isn't ready, then just leave it for a while and try again later when you see more signs of readiness. The more you push things, the worse they are likely to get.

Signs of readiness

Your child's behaviour will indicate when they are ready for your help in starting to use the potty or toilet. Signs of readiness include:

- Suddenly stopping what they are doing when they realise they need to wee or poo.
- Making a special movement, such as crossing legs, jiggling or squatting, just before they do a wee or poo.
- Making a particular noise, such as grunting or whining, when they need to go.
- Staying dry for a couple of hours at a time.
- Showing an interest when Mummy or Daddy go to the toilet.
- Having regular bowel movements, e.g. usually going for a poo after breakfast.
- Letting you know when they need changing.

When to start

When your child has shown signs of physical and psychological readiness, you can start to suggest that they use the potty. It helps to start during the summer months, when your child will naturally be running around with not much on. However, if your child shows signs of readiness during a cold spell, it's best to go with it then.

If there is a lot going on in other areas of your life or your child's life, you might want to delay for a bit, even if they are showing readiness. If you are already stressed with a new job or moving house, it's generally not a great idea to start potty training, as you might find it harder to be calm and patient. Similarly, if your child has just started nursery or has moved into a new bedroom, the last thing they need is another change.

How to introduce a potty

When supporting your child through any transition, it is always important to present the change as something exciting. The more positive you are, the more enthusiastic your child is likely to be.

Preparation

Buy the potty before you think you'll need it, so that it is on hand when your child starts to show signs of readiness. You could involve your child in choosing their own potty. Leave it in a visible place in the bathroom. Some parents buy two or more potties and place one on each floor or even in each room, for ease of access. When your child asks what it is, you can explain what it is for.

It can be helpful to introduce your child to pull-up nappies, also known as training pants, before you start potty training. Make sure they are wearing clothes that can easily be pulled up and down. Don't expect your child to negotiate tricky zips and buttons when they are rushing to get to the potty on time.

When your child starts to show signs of readiness, suggest that they might like to try using the potty. If you have the potty in the bathroom, you could use the toilet at the same time as your child uses the potty. This will often encourage them.

If they don't want to use it, leave it for a while. Never force your child to sit on the potty. They will naturally be curious about it. Wait for them to show signs that they want to use it. At first, they might just sit on it and not do anything. This is fine and is their way of getting used to it.

'When supporting your child through any transition, it is always important to present the change as something exciting. The more positive you are, the more enthusiastic your child is likely to be.'

Hygiene

Once your child has done a wee or poo on the potty, wipe them with some toilet paper or baby wipes. In time, you can encourage your child to start wiping themselves. It's best to check that their bottom is properly clean, after they've had a go. If you have a girl, make sure that you teach her the correct way to wipe herself from front to back.

Empty the contents of the potty in the toilet and flush it away, then wash out the potty with disinfectant. Some two-year-olds can be upset when they see their poo being flushed away. This can be because they see it as belonging to them and don't want to let it go!

This is quite a common reaction, so don't be alarmed. Gently explain that everyone's poo always gets flushed down the toilet and leave it at that. Be careful not to overdo the explanations about poo being dirty, as this can lead to your child developing feelings of shame.

Make sure you wash your hands afterwards, and get your child to wash their hands too, even if they haven't wiped themselves. This will help them to associate using the potty with hand washing from the outset.

Case study

Dawn's two-year-old son, Jesse, started showing an interest in using the potty without any prompting. Dawn and her husband decided not to rush Jesse but rather to let it happen naturally. Sometimes he would go in his nappy and at other times he would let them know he needed to 'go potty'.

Dawn noticed that if they allowed their son to go to the toilet by himself, he was more willing to use it on his own. She says, 'We have to allow him the chance to pull down his pants by himself, get on the seat by himself, flush the toilet by himself, and so on. This makes him feel like a "big boy" and instils confidence.'

However, Dawn has also noticed that if her son is in the bathroom by himself, he can get distracted by other things! So she keeps an eye out for clues that he will need to go and goes to the bathroom with him.

One step forward, two steps back

Once your child has started using the potty and shown that they are comfortable with it, you can gently prompt them to use it at regular intervals. Don't overdo it though. If you ask your child to sit on the potty every 10 minutes, they are likely to get fed up pretty quickly. Be sensible about it. You could ask before and/or after meals, naps and going out. Gradually, they will start to tell you when they want to go.

Always give your child lots of praise whenever they use the potty. Don't make a big deal of accidents. Even if you are calm and gentle, your child might still get upset if they wee in their pants or on the floor. Be as soothing as possible. Reassure them that it's okay and nothing to worry about, clean up any mess and get them into dry clothes without any fuss.

Learning any new skill takes time and practice. Although you may have heard of children potty training in a week, or even a weekend, this is not the normal state of affairs. Expect there to be clean days and messy days for a while. And if you find yourself mopping the living room floor for the 10th time in one day, always remember that you wore nappies once.

Once your child has started telling you when they need to use the potty, you can start leaving the nappies off during the day. You might want to keep them in pull-ups when you go out for a while longer.

Even if your child is progressing well on the potty, it is not uncommon for them to suddenly relapse, especially if they are under any stress. If there is a new baby in the household, your child has just started nursery or you have moved house, be prepared for a temporary blip in proceedings.

Graduating to the toilet

Once your child has mastered the potty, you can introduce the idea of the toilet. Some children prefer to skip the potty altogether and graduate straight to using the toilet. You can buy small training seats, which fit inside the standard toilet seat. Training seats can be wooden or plastic and some have extra padding for comfort.

'I'm not one of those parents who ask more than once if they need to go to the toilet before we leave home. I never did potty "training", so never got into the habit of asking. If he wants to go he'll go. I don't get these parents that force their kids to go or make them sit there "trying".'

Karen, mum to Bailey (aged two) and Leo (aged three).

A training seat can help your child feel more secure that they are not going to fall in the toilet. You can also buy a toddler step to help your child climb up onto the toilet. They may also like to hold onto the edge of the toilet seat at first and have you close at hand.

Your child might like you to stay very close by or they might ask you to turn around or leave the room, especially if they have observed this with others. Always respect their wishes when they ask for privacy.

Out and about

You will probably want to start leaving your child's nappy off inside the home before you do so out and about. You can leave your child in pull-ups or training pants when you go out and still encourage them to use the potty or toilet. Once you have stopped using nappies altogether, always remember to take a spare set or two of clothes out with you in case of accidents.

Consider taking the potty out with you in case you can't find a public toilet in time. You can buy specially designed travel potties, which fold up into a smaller size, and have liners which can be removed and the contents more easily thrown away.

Night time

Expect your child to take longer to stay dry at night than in the day. When they start regularly having dry nappies in the morning, you can consider leaving the nappy off at bedtime. You can buy washable or disposable mattress protector sheets to place under your child's sheet to cope with night time accidents.

A two-and-a-half-year-old cannot usually hold their wee for longer than four or five hours at a time, so they may need to get up in the night to use the potty or toilet. Your child is likely to want your help or simply your presence if they need to use the potty or toilet at night.

Some parents can find it helpful to semi wake their child and take them to the toilet just before the parents go to bed. However, it doesn't work for everyone and not all children can go on demand. If you try it and your child can't go or gets upset or cross, then it's best not to wake them in this way again.

'Expect your child to take longer to stay dry at night than in the day. When they start regularly having dry nappies in the morning, you can consider leaving the nappy off at bedtime.'

Summing Up

Most children are ready to start using a potty by the time they are two, but every child is different. Look for signs that your child is physically and psychologically ready before you introduce them to the potty.

Go gently and the process will be easier all round. The more relaxed you are about things, the less anxious your child will be. Like all key developmental milestones, there may be steps backwards as well as forwards. Try not to force things and be prepared for accidents.

About 90% of girls and 75% of boys can go without a nappy during the day by the age of two and a half. Don't worry if your child is later in using the potty. It's not a race.

Chapter Eight

Childcare and Early Education

Now is a good time to start thinking about playgroups, pre-schools and nurseries. These can help your child mix with other children and experience learning and development activities in addition to what you do with them at home.

Of course, if you (and your partner if you have one) are working, you may already be using childcare facilities. Or maybe you are thinking about returning to work after a period at home looking after your child.

Whatever your situation, now is a good time to review your childcare arrangements and think about any changes you might want to make.

Early years education

Funded places

Your child will usually be eligible for a funded part-time early years education place at a pre-school or nursery starting from the term after they turn three. If you want to take advantage of this provision, it's a good idea to start thinking about your options early on. There are often waiting lists for pre-schools and day nurseries.

Early learning

The Early Years Foundation Stage (EYFS) is a comprehensive framework which sets the standards for learning, development and care of children from birth to five.

EYFS sets out expected standards for all registered childcare settings. This includes childminders as well as pre-schools and nurseries.

Types of childcare

Childcare provision will vary from region to region, but the main choices are:

- Childminders.
- Playgroups.
- Pre-schools.
- Nurseries.

There are pros and cons to each option. You will need to weigh up what is being offered by various providers to find out how best to meet your child's needs and your own needs.

Making a choice

It is a good idea to visit any potential childcare providers during their opening hours so that you can see what children are doing in their care. If you like a particular service after visiting, arrange a second visit at a different time of day.

Take your child with you to see how the child carer reacts with them. When we were shopping around for child carers, I was shocked by some carers who made no attempt to interact with our son who was sitting in front of them. Also observe how your child responds to different people and environments.

Try to visit different types of childcare before you make a decision. Bear in mind that we can all sometimes unconsciously make decisions based on irrational factors. Try to keep an open mind. Even if you think you want a day nursery and are dead set against childminders, go and see at least one childminder too.

At the end of the day, trust your own judgement. What worked for your friends and their children may not necessarily be the best solution for your family. You know what you and your child need better than anyone else.

'We went to one nursery on many friends' recommendations, but it didn't work for us. After three weeks settling in, Etana wasn't having any of it! The second nursery was excellent and she's still there loving it! The staff are approachable and seem really happy in what they do, which makes a huge difference.'

Elaine, mum to Etana (aged three).

74

Legal issues

Registration and inspections

All childcare services in England must be registered with the Office for Standards in Education (OfSTED). The OfSTED equivalent in Scotland is HM Inspectorate of Education (HMIE). Estyn is the office of Her Majesty's Inspectorate for Education and Training in Wales. In Northern Ireland, responsibility rests with the Department for Education Northern Ireland (DENI).

When you visit a childminder's home or a pre-school or nursery, always ask to look at their inspection report.

Contracts

Whichever type of childcare you use, you will need to sign a legally binding contract that will cover hours, fees, closures/sickness/holiday pay, settling in terms and notice periods. Make sure that the contract does not tie you into a long notice period.

If you are presented with any terms or conditions that you don't feel comfortable agreeing to, do say so and see if they can be renegotiated.

Childminders

Registered childminders are self-employed and look after children in their own home. They are allowed to care for up to six children under the age of eight (including their own), but only three of them can be aged under five.

If you want your child to be cared for in a family home and have one consistent carer, then a childminder is a good option. If you have a job with irregular hours, you may find that a childminder is more accommodating than a day nursery. Using a childminder can be particularly helpful if you have more than one child and want them to be cared for together.

If you don't want your child to miss out on pre-school or nursery facilities, remember that childminders can drop your child off at a pre-school or nursery session and then pick them up later. That way you and your child can get the best of both worlds.

Childminders are self-employed, which means that they decide on working hours and fees. You will need to negotiate hours, terms and conditions together. Although they may be more flexible than day nurseries, they can also be less reliable as they will not usually arrange cover if they are sick or go on holiday. Make sure you are clear on what is being offered before you commit.

A childminder's home must meet certain safety guidelines and they are required to attend basic training (including first aid) before they can register with OfSTED. Some may hold or be working towards formal childcare qualifications but this is not required. Any adults living in the childminder's home will also be police checked. OfSTED will inspect your childminder at home on a regular basis.

Before you decide

Ask what the childminder offers and talk through your needs and your child's needs. Make sure you have a look at their policies and seek references from satisfied parents. Agree on key issues around meal times, activities, watching television and behaviour management.

Pre-schools and playgroups

Pre-schools or playgroups provide care and learning for children between two and a half and five years old. They operate on a part-time basis, offering morning or afternoon sessions, usually during term time only. Some of the staff will hold childcare qualifications and others may be working towards them.

Pre-schools may be privately run. Alternatively, they may be delivered by community or voluntary groups on a not-for-profit basis, often with help from parents, in which case fees are likely to be cheaper.

The advantage of using a pre-school or playgroup rather than a childminder is that your child will be mixing with other children of a similar age. They are also likely to have access to a wider range of toys, equipment and activities.

If you need full day care, you could arrange for a childminder to drop off and collect your child from pre-school and to look after your child during the school holidays.

Before you decide

Facilities offered at playgroups and pre-schools vary enormously, so make sure you ask about the kinds of things your child will be doing. Have a look at the toys and resources available and the indoor and outdoor space that your child can use.

Nursery

You may wish to consider enrolling your child at a nursery class when they turn three. They could either attend a school nursery or a day nursery.

Remember that your child will usually be eligible for a funded part-time place at a pre-school or nursery starting from the term after they turn three, so you should not need to pay for a part-time nursery place regardless of provider.

If your child is already in a day nursery for longer hours, you can continue with this service and just pay for fewer hours.

School nursery

State school nurseries offer free early years education for children from the age of three, and usually offer either morning or afternoon sessions. If you would like your child to go to a school nursery class, you must apply direct to the school. It is a good idea to visit first.

Unlike private services, school nurseries do not usually offer places on the basis of length of time on the waiting list. Priority is usually given to parents and carers who live, with their children, in the local authority. You will usually need to supply proof of where you and your child live.

Day nursery

Private 'day nurseries' are open for longer hours than school nurseries, and usually provide a service from 8am to 6pm on weekdays, for 50 weeks of the year. Most day nurseries will offer full- or part-time places. There must be one adult to every four two-year-olds (with lower adult:child ratios for older children).

Before you decide

Check out the daily routine for meals, play and nap times, and make sure that these will work for your child. Ask whether your child will be assigned their own particular key member of staff and find out how much continuity of care there is.

Securing a place

Whatever service you choose, make sure you put your child's name down for a place as soon as possible. There are often waiting lists for pre-school and playgroups. Even if you're not yet ready for childcare, it's a good idea to start looking sooner rather than later.

You will normally be asked to pay a refundable deposit to secure a place (not applicable for state nursery school). You may also be asked to sign a contract at this stage.

Settling in visits

Leaving your child with somebody new is a big step for both of you. It is particularly momentous if this is the first time they have been cared for by someone other than family.

It is important that you plan a sensible settling in period to make the transition as stress-free as possible. Even if you are only changing from one provider to another, such as a childminder to a nursery, you will still need to allow a period of settling in for your child.

'So my baby girl is going to start nursery and I think I am more apprehensive than she is. All she knows is that she will be going in the car and she loves the car ... but wait until she sees me walk out of the nursery gates and leave her behind, she will not be impressed.'

Samantha, mum to Nia (aged two).

If your child is starting childcare because you are going back to work, start the settling in well in advance so that you both feel confident and ready in time. Stay with your child the first few times, staying in the background for the last visit.

If possible, leave your child for a very short period, such as an hour, to see how they respond and then build up the time spent away from them. Once you are ready to leave the premises, don't hang about or look anxious as they will pick up on this. Stay upbeat and tell them where you are going and when you are coming back. Even though they won't fully understand time, it will help your child know what to expect.

Try not to rush the settling in period. More time invested now will save stress later.

Case study

Samantha spent a week at the nursery with her daughter Nia, getting her used to the environment, the staff and the other children. The first day that Samantha had to leave Nia for the whole day, she said she was tempted to sneak away while she was playing but was advised that it's not a good idea as it can have adverse effects on children regarding trust.

Samantha knew that Nia would cry when she left but still found it very difficult. The staff invited Samantha to call back and check on Nia. When Samantha called back an hour later, Nia was still crying, and when she called an hour after that she was still crying on and off.

The nursery reassured Samantha that Nia would settle in eventually and that she could call as many times as she wanted. When Samantha went to collect Nia at the end of her first day, she could see from her face that she had been crying most of the day.

This went on for the whole week, although the crying became less and less and Nia actually settled very quickly. For the first term, she only did three days a week, as Samantha felt that it would be too much of a drastic move to send her full time, five days a week straightaway. Nia now attends daily from 8am to 3pm and goes off happily in the morning.

First day

Your child's first full day in a childcare setting is likely to be a little daunting for both of you. A good settling in period will help alleviate the stress, but still be prepared for a few tears on the first day – and that's just you!

Talk positively to your child about their first day and what they will be doing. Try to arrange a treat to mark their first day or week, perhaps a special outing or a present.

'Each morning, I would talk to her as I got her dressed and explain that she was going to nursery and was going to play with her new friends and play in the garden.'

Samantha, mum to Nia (aged two).

Parental involvement

Most day nurseries, playgroups and pre-schools welcome parental involvement. This can be by responding to parent consultation, contributing ideas or (if you are able to) going in and helping out with the children. Talk to staff about ways in which you can be involved.

Some parents may like to go in and help out with an activity, such as baking, or read a story to a group of children. Tell the staff about any special interests or skills that you have and how you might be able to share these with the children. Childminders may also welcome parents' input more informally.

Avoiding and resolving problems

If you are worried about anything that is happening with your child carer, talk through your concerns as soon as possible to nip things in the bud and work through your worries.

The best ways to avoid problems escalating are:

- Being clear about expectations at the outset.
- Letting the service know in advance if you anticipate that you might need to make any changes to your arrangements.
- Establishing regular parent-childcare communication.
- Talking through any worries with your child carer as soon as they arise.

- Keeping an open mind about possible resolutions to any problems that do crop up.

- Trying not to be defensive if your child carer asks you about how you do things at home.

Communicating with childcare providers

Many childcare providers will have their own communication systems, such as a daily record sheet or parents' book that they send home with your child. This will typically tell you:

- What your child has eaten and when.

- The time and length of any naps.

- Details of nappy changes, toilet training and accidents.

- Some information about the activities that they have been doing.

Nurseries, playgroups and pre-schools may also provide newsletters with updates about activities as well as opportunities for parents to get involved.

'The nursery always try to help by squeezing us in if I get called into work or letting me drop her off a little earlier than the session starts, so I can get to work on time. Any problems I have had have always been dealt with quickly. '

Elaine, mum to Etana (aged three).

Summing Up

You will probably want to start thinking about childcare provision some time during your child's second year. This will help provide social experiences, as well as new learning and development activities for your child.

Even if your child is already cared for by someone else while you work, it is still a good time to review available nursery and pre-school provision well before they approach three.

The main choices are childminders, playgroups, pre-schools and day nurseries. Be sure to shop around and visit services more than once before you commit yourselves. Be clear on expectations and needs at the outset to avoid problems.

A well-planned settling in period can make the transition to day care easier all round. Keeping the lines of communication open with your child's carer will help to prevent any problems from occurring and quickly resolve any that do arise.

Chapter Nine

Siblings

Thinking about having another child?

It is quite common to start thinking about having a second child when your first child is around two. In many ways this makes a lot of sense – your first child is moving away from babyhood and starting to become more independent, yet the children will be close enough in age to be able to benefit from playing together.

Many people take the plunge sooner and have two children under two – you will hear from one such mum, Mariam, shortly. Other chapters feature case studies with Shannon and Marianne, mums with twins, who got the second child dilemma out of the way from day one!

Perhaps you already have older children and your two-year-old is the youngest in the family. Maybe you have decided not to have any more children, an equally valid option. We will look at all these permutations in this chapter.

Interesting fact

The greatest recorded number of children ever born to one woman is a staggering 69!

The first wife of Feodor Vassilyev of Russia gave birth to 16 pairs of twins, seven sets of triplets and four sets of quadruplets in 27 pregnancies in the 17th century. Only two of her children died at infancy.

Source: www.newvision.co.ug.

Age gaps

There is no perfect time to have a second child. It will depend on your individual circumstances – your and your partner's age and health, your relationship, your financial situation, your lifestyle and your first child's needs.

The natural advantage of having two children close in age is that they will be able to do more things together than if you have, say, a six-year-old and a baby. The disadvantage, of course, is that generally speaking the younger the child, the more intense the work involved.

You might be keen to get the nappies and night feeds out of the way all in one go. Or you might prefer to wait until your first child is in nursery or school before having a second baby, so that you will have time alone with the baby during the day.

Case study

Mariam and her husband John chose to try for their second baby when their son Lewis was just nine months old. They had experienced difficulties conceiving the first time round because of Mariam's endometriosis. At a routine scan, Mariam was advised that if she wanted a second baby, now would be an ideal time before the endometriosis returned.

Lewis was only 18 months when Charlie was born. Mariam says that it was a distinct advantage still being in baby mode when Charlie was born. The family still had a lot of Lewis's baby clothes and toys for Charlie to use, although, of course, she got more than her fair share of new stuff too.

A major plus for Mariam was getting all the nappies and night feeds out of the way in one go. And because of when their birthdays fell, the children started school within a year of each other.

Preparing your child for a baby brother or sister

Young children are fascinated by the whole idea of pregnancy and new babies. They will ask questions and often role play at being pregnant themselves, regardless of whether they are a boy or girl.

Involving your child

It is a good idea to prepare your child for the new arrival while you are pregnant. Involve your child by explaining that the baby is in your belly. Let them stroke your bump and talk to the baby.

If you decide to find out the sex of your unborn baby, it can be a good idea to tell your child whether they are having a brother or sister. Telling your child that they have a new baby brother waiting in your tummy to come out and meet them can make it more real for them.

They can also 'help' you get things ready, such as the new baby's room. Explain what you are doing with each task, e.g. 'This is where your new sister is going to sleep', or 'These are some little clothes for your new brother'.

You could also involve your child in discussing possible names for the new baby. But don't be surprised if they want to call the baby Igglepiggle or something equally ridiculous.

The important thing is to talk to your child about the idea of having a brother or sister. It will still be a shock to find that they are no longer the centre of attention, but at least you have given them some forewarning.

'It was hard going at times having two kids under two, but I wouldn't have it any other way. I couldn't imagine starting all over again with a new baby when the first one starts school!'

Mariam, mum to Lewis (aged seven) and Charlie (aged five).

Coping with jealousy

No matter how excited your child is about the arrival of a little brother or sister, it is inevitable that they will experience feelings of jealousy too. This is completely normal and natural. You can't stop your child being jealous but by preparing them beforehand and making a fuss of them when the new baby arrives, you can help them to cope.

'No matter how excited your child is about the arrival of a little brother or sister, it is inevitable that they will experience feelings of jealousy too. This is completely normal and natural.'

Sharing

If you are recycling some of your child's old clothes and toys for the baby, be prepared for them to become territorial and scream 'Mine!' when they catch sight of their old baby gym. They may well have turned their nose up at it over a year ago, but it will suddenly seem like the most desirable toy on the planet!

Remember that if they are the first child, they have never had to share their own things in this way before. Even if they are used to mixing with other children, they will not be used to their toys suddenly belonging to someone else.

When the new baby arrives, your child will have to learn to share in a different way to how they share with their friends. Fundamentally, they are learning to share their mummy and daddy with another small person and that can be hard to take!

How you can help

It can help if you buy your child a special present or let them choose a new toy to replace the toys that they are giving the baby. You can also involve your child in buying their own gift for the baby at the same time.

It is also important to recognise and acknowledge your child's feelings rather than deny them. It can be hard to face up to the fact that when you are out of the room, your child may be poking the baby or behaving in a way that could hurt the baby. But it is better to anticipate this.

It is generally not a good idea to leave a young child alone with a new baby sibling. Your new baby will need protecting from possible harm, even if it is accidental. Equally, your young child will need protecting from their own feelings of jealousy, which could lead them to act in a hostile way towards the baby.

Older siblings

You may already have older children and have decided not to have any more, in which case your two-year-old will be the youngest. Some parents in this situation can find it hard to stop seeing their youngest as the baby. You may find yourself treating your youngest child very differently from the way you treated your eldest when they turned two.

Only child

Of course you may decide, for whatever reason, that although you love being a parent to your beloved two-year-old, you just don't want to have any more children, or perhaps it is not possible. Or maybe you are simply not ready to make the decision quite yet.

Interesting fact

Only child families represent:

17% of families in Britain.

50% of families in Germany and Portugal.

100% of families in China (since the one child policy of 1979).

Source: www.beinganonly.com.

According to Ann Richardson, founder of Beinganonly.com, being an only child is not better or worse than having siblings, just different. There will be advantages and disadvantages and every only child's experience will be different.

Pros and cons

Richardson argues that some adult onlies feel that they have developed many positive personal qualities through their experience of being an only child. This includes being: capable, reliable, a good friend to others, sensitive, thoughtful, considerate, organised and responsible.

The obvious advantage of being an only child is that a child receives a lot of one-to-one attention from their parents. Only children often tend to be more mature in their outlook and become resourceful in entertaining themselves.

The downside is that this can sometimes be lonely, and too much parental attention can sometimes be stifling. They can miss having siblings to play with and to support one another in adult years.

Supporting an only child

If your child is an only child or even a first child, it is important to give them plenty of opportunities to mix with other children. This could be something as simple as dropping into the local playground, or by taking your child to more structured environments such as playgroups, pre-schools and nurseries, as discussed in the previous chapter.

As your child gets older, it is helpful for them to have the opportunity to see the same children over a period of time to develop friendships. Perhaps you have friends or relatives with children who would be happy to agree to regular play dates. Young children often enjoy mixing with older children, as well as those their own age.

Summing Up

You might be thinking of having a second child, or perhaps you already have a new baby or older children. Alternatively, it may be that your two-year-old is likely to be an only child, either through choice or necessity.

If you do have another child, it is important to prepare your first child for the arrival of a new baby brother or sister, and to have realistic expectations of them when their sibling arrives.

If your child is an only or first child, make sure that you provide them with opportunities to mix with other children so they can develop their social skills.

Chapter 10

Seeking Help

Getting help when you need it

We all have times when we need a little help. It is important to remember that seeking help is not a sign of weakness. Rather it shows that you are being sensible and proactive in working to overcome challenges. We are not superhuman and no one is perfect. We do not always have the answers.

A support network

Family and friends can provide a valuable support network. Friends who have known you for a long time, from before you were a parent, know you as a person, not just little Tommy or Anna's mum or dad, and can help put things into perspective.

Sometimes, however, you really need to talk to another parent, someone who's been there, done that, worn the t-shirt and got the sick down it! Here, parent and toddler groups and other such networks can be great ways of meeting other parents. Online parenting forums are also becoming an increasingly popular way to chat.

However, sometimes it can help to talk to someone outside of your immediate circle, someone who doesn't know you at all. You might want to speak to someone in confidence, someone who will be non-judgemental. And, of course, there are some matters for which you really do need to seek professional help.

'They never tell you that it's this hard. It's hard to get them to sleep through the night. It's hard to get them through toddlerhood. I'm proud and happy and overjoyed I had children. Sometimes, though, I just wish it was a little bit easier.'

Shannon, mum to Nick and Nora, twins (aged two).

Case study

Shannon is mum to two-year-old twins, Nick and Nora.

Shannon has been blogging since before she had children. Since having her twins, she often blogs about the ups and downs of motherhood.

Most of the time, she appreciates the advice and encouragement from fellow bloggers posting comments on her entries. Other parents can often offer practical advice and tips that she had not considered before.

However, she also gets comments telling her how she should do things and what she's doing incorrectly. She says she often wants to talk about her children but feels like she has to defend herself vigorously in doing so.

Shannon says she no longer wants to censor herself for fear of judgement. After all, we all raise our children differently and it is important to be true to yourself.

Visit Shannon's blog at www.everydaystranger.net.

Seeking outside help

There are many different reasons why parents of young children may need to seek outside help. You might need help because:

- You are concerned about an aspect of your child's health. Perhaps their eczema is escalating and you want some advice.

- You are worried about their eating habits. Perhaps they have suddenly stopped eating certain foods and you are worried.

- You have questions about other aspects of their development. Perhaps you feel you need some extra advice on potty training.

- You are having financial difficulties and want advice on financial support that may be available. Perhaps you are looking to return to work after a period of staying at home to look after your child.

- You are finding it difficult to cope and want some emotional support. Perhaps you are exhausted because your child isn't sleeping well. It is very common to feel overwhelmed from time to time and is absolutely nothing to be ashamed of.

Where to get help

Help is available from a range of sources, depending on the type of help you need. Contact details for useful organisations are listed in the help list. One very useful starting place is the UK charity called Home-Start, which offers befriending and practical help to families with under fives. Local branches can match you and your family with a trained volunteer. I have inside-out knowledge of their services – I worked for them as a volunteer and personally received support when my son was a colicky baby, and I needed an extra pair of hands and a chat to remain sane.

Types of help

There are many different types of help available. These include:

- Information – this could be from books, magazines, websites, helplines or information services.

- Professional advice – this may include medical advice from a doctor or advice from other professionals such as a paediatrician or health visitor.

- Befriending – you may find it helpful to meet with other parents to share worries and experiences for reassurance and tips. This type of help can be invaluable and should never be underestimated.

- Practical help – you may want someone to help you in a practical way, either around the house or out and about. Perhaps you'd like someone to go with you and your child to the swimming pool, or help you out with shopping.

- Emotional support – you might just want someone to talk to, who can listen in a supportive, non-judgemental way. This could be a befriender or someone who is trained in listening and/or counselling skills.

'I have met lots of good friends through parenting and I'm glad to say we are all so different but we respect each other's lifestyles and choices. Children are individuals too. I don't know any kid that is a textbook kid. They don't exist!'

Elaine, mum to Etana (aged three).

- Special needs – if you or your child has a disability, serious illness or other type of special need, you may be able to get practical support from social services. There are also charities that can offer help in these situations (see help list).

Your GP

'There are times when you do something and think, "The Mummy Police are coming for me when they hear about this." No one judges as hard as another parent. Not even the UK Home Office, and that's saying something.'

Shannon, mum to Nick and Nora, twins (aged two).

Your GP will usually be your first point of call for any health issues for you or your child. Your GP can make a diagnosis, prescribe treatment or make a referral to another service or specialist.

Referrals

Your GP is, in some ways, the gatekeeper to a range of health services. You will often need a GP referral to get to see another health professional.

A GP will sometimes refer a child to a paediatrician if there are health concerns that fall outside of their expertise. A paediatrician (often called a neonatologist) is a doctor specialising in child health.

Your health visitor

All families with children under five have a named health visitor. A health visitor helps families to stay healthy. They can offer advice on a range of matters, including feeding, sleeping, growth and development.

You can find their contact details in your 'little red book', which would have been issued to you soon after your baby was born. Alternatively, contact your local health centre or children's centre. They may offer drop-in sessions or appointment-only services.

Children's centres

In England and Wales, children's centres offer a one-stop shop for services for families with young children. Services available vary from centre to centre but may include:

- Health visitor services.
- Parenting advice.
- Information on childcare options.
- Early education and childcare.

Contact your local council for details of your nearest children's centre.

Things operate a little differently in Scotland and Northern Ireland, although services for parents-to-be and families are still provided in the community according to local need. Ask your health visitor what is available in your area or see the relevant websites listed in the help list.

Questioning the 'experts'

Whether consulting a health professional or reading an advice guide, it is important to remember that the views of experts are not gospel. There are usually a range of different schools of thought relating to any one issue. It is up to you to decide what parenting ideas and approaches work best for you and your family. It is okay to question the experts.

Cultural context

Social norms and parenting practices vary according to culture and social context. For example, in some cultures it is normal to co-sleep with babies, toddlers and older children, whereas in Western society this is often frowned upon.

Trust yourself. If something feels wrong to you, according to your own personal values, beliefs and world view, then don't do it. Conversely, if you discover an approach that feels right for your family, follow your instincts. You don't have to do what everyone else is doing!

Current thinking

'Current thinking' is also just that. It is what 'experts' advise at a particular time based on the available research and information. Experts are not infallible and their thinking changes. Consider that your own ideas might sometimes be ahead of the game.

When my son was a baby, dummies were frowned upon by health visitors. They could supposedly affect, among other things, speech, teeth and emotional attachments, or so they said. I spent ages trying to wean him off the thing. When I finally did so, new government advice was issued recommending the use of a dummy up to six months, following research that showed that it helped reduce the risk of cot death. Oh, how I howled.

Throw away the rules

Despite what some childcare manuals would like you to believe, there are no rules when it comes to how to parent. One size cannot fit all. Methods are sometimes presented as 'The Gospel' rather than simply the ideas put forward by an individual or group based on their particular view of the world.

What I have tried to do in this book is to present you with options and ideas. What you decide to do with this information is entirely up to you. I would encourage you to question everything.

Avoiding burnout

Everyone agrees that looking after young children, though hugely rewarding, is also extremely exhausting and, at times, stressful. Whether you are at home with your toddler full time or you are a working parent, there will undoubtedly be times when you feel overwhelmed. It is important not to get to the stage when you feel completely burnt out because then you will be no good to anyone!

'I have just been to see my GP, where I surprised myself by becoming quite tearful during the consultation. I'd noticed for some time I had been sleeping badly, and that my concentration when playing with the Emperor was not good.'

Caroline Dunford, author of *How to Survive the Terrible Twos: Diary of a Mother Under Siege.*

In her fascinating real life account, *How to Survive the Terrible Twos: Diary of a Mother Under Siege,* Caroline Dunford recounts how she and her GP came to the conclusion that she needed to start spending some time away from her two-year-old. This was important both to prepare him for starting nursery at three, and also to meet her own needs outside of the parenting role.

Top tips for avoiding burnout

- Talk to other parents to share problems and find new ideas that might help you and your family. This could include participating in online parenting forums, as well as meeting people face to face.

- Remember that although your child is your number one priority, your needs are important too. Don't feel guilty for wanting to have time away from your child. This is perfectly normal.

- Make sure you take time to relax and do things you enjoy when your child is asleep in the evening. Simple things, such as having a hot bath with candles, reading a magazine or novel in bed, or watching a programme that you enjoy on television, can all help. When you are stressed out, problems can seem insurmountable. When you take time to nurture yourself, you will gain perspective and start to feel more positive. Some parents find meditation exercises helpful.

- Schedule in regular time out from parenting (and work) to pursue an interest or activity. Classes can be good as the routine encourages you to continue going. If you have a partner, negotiate an arrangement that works for you both. For example, I attend a weekly Pilates session and my husband knows that this time is sacrosanct! If you are a single parent, rope in friends or family or find a trusted babysitter. You might be able to come up with a regular reciprocal arrangement with other parents.

- Find time to socialise both as a parent and outside of your parenting role. A girl's night out or boy's night out with friends can work wonders. If you have a partner, it is important to have time together as a couple, as well as spending time together as a family. This can be something as simple as sharing a romantic meal together at home when your child is in bed. Going out together on a 'date' can also be fun.

Summing Up

Being a parent of a two-year-old can be hard work. We all have times when we need a little help. Developing a support network can be invaluable in avoiding burnout. There are also a range of different avenues to pursue if you feel you need outside help at any time.

Remember that it is okay to question 'the experts'. It is up to you to decide what parenting ideas and approaches work best for you and your family.

I hope this book has proved to be a useful guide and has given you some ideas and inspiration to help you as a parent of a terrific two-year-old.

You may find these Need2Know titles useful, as they cover specific issues touched on in this guide:

- *Special Educational Needs – A Parent's Guide.*
- *Working Mothers – The Essential Guide.*
- *Single Parents – The Essential Guide.*
- *Allergies – A Parent's Guide.*
- *Children's Nutrition – A Parent's Guide.*
- *Travelling with Children – A Parent's Guide.*
- *Fatherhood – The Essential Guide.*
- *Primary School – A Parent's Guide.*

Help List

Attachment Parenting International

www.attachmentparenting.org
Parenting website and forum. Information on co-sleeping and the other principles of attachment parenting can be found here.

Being An Only

www.beinganonly.com
Website and web community dedicated to being an only child.

Contact a Family

Tel: 0800 808 3555 (helpline)
helpline@cafamily.org.uk
www.cafamily.org.uk
UK charity providing support, advice and information for families with disabled children.

Department for Education (NI)

www.deni.gov.uk
Northern Ireland's education department website. You'll find information on inspection of childcare services on this site.

DirectGov

www.direct.gov.uk
Government information website. Lots of information can be found about parenting and childcare. There is a search facility in the childcare section to find local childcare provisions.

Disability, Pregnancy and Parenthood International (DPPI)

Tel: 0800 018 4730

info@dppi.org.uk

www.dppi.org.uk

UK information charity for disabled parents, and the publisher of the international journal on disabled parenting, *Disability, Pregnancy and Parenthood International*.

Estyn

www.estyn.gov.uk

Her Majesty's Inspectorate for Education and Training in Wales. You'll find information on inspection of childcare services on this site.

HM Inspectorate of Education

www.hmie.gov.uk

You'll find information on inspection of childcare services in Scotland on this site.

Home-Start

Tel: 0822 068 63 68 (infoline)

www.home-start.org.uk

A national charity with local schemes of volunteers throughout the UK offering support and practical help to parents with children under the age of five.

Mumsnet

www.mumsnet.com

Website that aims to make parents' lives easier by pooling knowledge, experience and support.

Netmums

www.netmums.com

A family of local sites that cover the UK, each site offering information to mothers on everything from where to find playgroups and how to eat healthily, to where to meet other mothers.

NI Direct

www.nidirect.gov.uk
Northern Ireland public services website including a search facility for childcare providers. Click on 'parents' to access the relevant section.

OfSTED

www.ofsted.gov.uk
You'll find information on inspection of childcare services in England on this site.

Parentline Plus

Tel: 0808 800 222
www.parentlineplus.org.uk
A national charity offering help and support for parents through an innovative range of free, flexible, responsive services.

Scottish Childcare

www.scottishchildcare.gov.uk
One-stop shop for childcare information in Scotland.

Welsh Assembly Government

www.wales.gov.uk
Welsh public services website including a search facility for childcare providers. Click on 'children and young people' to access the parenting section of the website.

Zero to Three

www.zerotothree.org
A not-for-profit organisation in the US that informs, trains and supports parents, professionals and policymakers to improve the lives of infants.

Book List

Birth to Five
By the Department of Health, 2009.
Free guide for parents in England, Wales and Northern Ireland.
Available online at: www.nhs.uk/planners/birthtofive.

Einstein Never Used Flash Cards: How Our Children Really Learn – And Why They Need to Play More and Memorize Less
By Kathy Hirsh-Pasek, Roberta Michnick Golinkoff and Diane Eyer, Rodale Books, USA, 2003.

How to Survive the Terrible Twos: Diary of a Mother Under Siege
By Caroline Dunford, White Ladder Press, Great Ambrook, 2005.

New Babycare Book: A Practical Guide to the First Three Years
By Miriam Stoppard, Dorling Kindersley, London, 2002.

The No-Cry Sleep Solution for Toddlers and Preschoolers
By Elizabeth Pantley, McGraw Hill, New York, 2005.

On Becoming A Person
By Carl Rogers, Houghton Mifflin, Boston, 1961.

Ready Steady Toddler
By Health Scotland, 2007.
Free guide for parents in Scotland.
Available online at: www.readysteadytoddler.org.uk.

The Sleep Book for Tired Parents
By Rebecca Huntley, Souvenir Press Ltd, London, 1992.

Understanding Your Two-Year-Old
By Lisa Miller, Jessica Kingsley Publishers, London, 2006.

Winning Parent, Winning Child: Parenting So That Everybody Wins
By Jan Fortune-Wood, Cinnamon Press, Gwynedd, 2005.

Need2Know

References

Being an Only, *Being an Only Child*, 2004, www.beinganonly.com/beinganonly.html, accessed 26 July 2010.

Maslow, A H, 'A Theory of Human Motivation', *Psychological Review*, 1927, vol. 50, pages 370-96.

Pavlov, I P, *Conditioned Reflexes: An Investigation of the Physiological Activity of the Cerebral Cortex* (translated and edited by GV Anrep), Oxford University Press, London, 1943.

Pentley, E, *The No-Cry Sleep Solution for Toddlers and Preschoolers*, McGraw Hill, New York, 2005.

Smith, P and Biggins, R, *The Trouble with 21st Century Kids*, SPI Play, Wrexham, 2006.

Tannock, MT, Lyons, CD and Sileo, NM, 'Rough-and-Tumble Play of Infants and Toddlers: Supporting Development and Family Connections'. In *Zero to Three Conference*, Los Angeles, 5 December 2008. Zero to Three, Washington DC, 2008.

The New Vision, *Factfile on the world's highest births,* 2005, www.newvision.co.ug/D/9/31/446825, accessed 10 June 2010.

Need -2- Know

Need - 2 - Know

Available Titles Include ...

Allergies A Parent's Guide
ISBN 978-1-86144-064-8 £8.99

Autism A Parent's Guide
ISBN 978-1-86144-069-3 £8.99

Drugs A Parent's Guide
ISBN 978-1-86144-043-3 £8.99

Dyslexia and Other Learning Difficulties
A Parent's Guide ISBN 978-1-86144-042-6 £8.99

Bullying A Parent's Guide
ISBN 978-1-86144-044-0 £8.99

Epilepsy The Essential Guide
ISBN 978-1-86144-063-1 £8.99

Teenage Pregnancy The Essential Guide
ISBN 978-1-86144-046-4 £8.99

Gap Years The Essential Guide
ISBN 978-1-86144-079-2 £8.99

How to Pass Exams A Parent's Guide
ISBN 978-1-86144-047-1 £8.99

Child Obesity A Parent's Guide
ISBN 978-1-86144-049-5 £8.99

Applying to University The Essential Guide
ISBN 978-1-86144-052-5 £8.99

ADHD The Essential Guide
ISBN 978-1-86144-060-0 £8.99

Student Cookbook - Healthy Eating The Essential Guide
ISBN 978-1-86144-061-7 £8.99

Stress The Essential Guide
ISBN 978-1-86144-054-9 £8.99

Adoption and Fostering A Parent's Guide
ISBN 978-1-86144-056-3 £8.99

Special Educational Needs A Parent's Guide
ISBN 978-1-86144-057-0 £8.99

The Pill An Essential Guide
ISBN 978-1-86144-058-7 £8.99

University A Survival Guide
ISBN 978-1-86144-072-3 £8.99

Diabetes The Essential Guide
ISBN 978-1-86144-059-4 £8.99

View the full range at www.need2knowbooks.co.uk. To order our titles, call **01733 898103**, email **sales@n2kbooks.com** or visit the website.

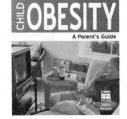

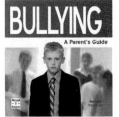

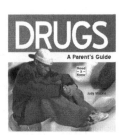

Need - 2 - Know, Remus House, Coltsfoot Drive, Peterborough, PE2 9JX